Spain travel guide:

an unusual and evocative journey across Spain

By Penelope Arias & Francesco Umbria

© **Copyright 2019 - All rights reserved.**

The content contained within this book may not be reproduced, duplicated or transmitted without direct written permission from the author or the publisher.

Under no circumstances will any blame or legal responsibility be held against the publisher, or author, for any damages, reparation, or monetary loss due to the information contained within this book. Either directly or indirectly.

Legal Notice:

This book is copyright protected. This book is only for personal use. You cannot amend, distribute, sell, use, quote or paraphrase any part, or the content within this book, without the consent of the author or publisher.

Disclaimer Notice:

Please note the information contained within this document is for educational and entertainment purposes only. All effort has been executed to present accurate, up to date, and reliable, complete information.

No warranties of any kind are declared or implied. Readers acknowledge that the author is not engaging in the rendering of legal, financial, medical or professional advice.

The content within this book has been derived from various sources. Please consult a licensed professional before attempting any techniques outlined in this book.

By reading this document, the reader agrees that under no circumstances is the author responsible for any losses, direct or indirect, which are incurred as a result of the use of information contained within this document, including, but not limited to, — errors, omissions, or inaccuracies.

Table of Contents

Introduction _____ 5

Chapter 1: Well? _____ 6

Chapter 2: Oh My! _____ 44

Chapter 3: Check Out the Spots _____ 69

Chapter 4: What Else to Notice? _____ 99

Acknowledgements _____ 143

Bonus chapter: _____ 144

Introduction

Congratulations on purchasing *Spain travel guide: an unusual and evocative journey across Spain* and thank you for doing so.

The following chapters will discuss different parts of Spain.

There are plenty of books on this subject on the market, thanks again for choosing this one! Every effort was made to ensure it is full of as much useful information as possible, please enjoy!

Chapter 1: Well?

Sevilla's Sacred Week (Semana Santa Clause) festivities act as Spain's most amazing. In the course of the week paving the way to Easter, the whole place is pressed with pioneers seeing 50 parades conveying around a hundred religious buoys. In case you're here outside that week, you can at present figure out this occasion by going to the Basílica de la Macarena (worked in the late 1940's) just to witness the two incredible buoys and the sweetheart of Blessed Week, Sobbing Virgin.

This Mary comes total with precious stone tears — she resembles a seventeenth century doll dressed in arms and natural hair and explained arms, and also put on the underclothes. The delightful articulation — somewhere in between grinning and wailing— is making a move in an Ornate way. Her sobbing can be infectious; guests who come to see her are frequently moved to tears. Filling a close by side church is the Sentence's Christ, demonstrating Christ during the time in which he was denounced.

The 2 highly significant buoys of the Blessed Week marches — the buoys that Jesus and Mary rode each Great Friday — were likewise in this congregation, stopped behind the raised area (these require a historical center pass to see).

The 3-ton skim, which conveys Jesus is dressed in leaf with the golden color, and demonstrates a disturbance of, makes sense of condemning of Jesus, who was set way ahead of this group). The presiding judge is going to get out of the whole case. Pilate's significant other woes as a normal man peruse capital punishment. While devout Sevillan ladies moan in the boulevards, transfers of 48 men convey this buoy — with just the feet appearing beneath the window hangings — as they mix via the lanes from 12 PM to 2 PM. each Great Friday.

La Esperanza pursues the Condemning of Christ within the parade. The littler (1.5-ton) coast of Mary, in a close by room, seems to be all candles and silver— "sufficiently able to help the rooftop yet delicate enough to tremble in the delicate night breeze." Mary posses a closet of 3 enormous shawls that are worn in progressive years, and each is shown here. The enormous green mantle has its roots back in 1900. Her 6-pound golden crown/radiance came was first unveiled in 1913. It mesmerizingly affects the neighborhood swarms. Individuals line awake for hours, applauding, sobbing, and tossing roses as the buoy gradually operates in the city. My Sevillan companion clarified, "She knows every one of the issues of Sevilla and its kin. We've been trusting in her for a considerable length of time. To us she is trust. That is her name — Esperanza."

The historical center zone additionally has an instance of bullfighter outfits, which were offered to the congregation throughout the years by matadors, in much obliged for the insurance. Thought about the defender of matadors, Macerena is enormous in various churches. In the early 1900's, she was offered 5 emerald ornaments she puts on by the matador José Ortega. It was in operation for eight years...up to the time he was gutted to the ultimate death within the ring. It was a major ordeal, which she was wearing dark a short time later — the main time that has occurred.)

Outside the congregation you can see the best enduring piece of Sevilla's old dividers. Initially Roman, the only remainder today is twelfth century Moorish, an update that for a considerable length of time. What's more, truly, it is also from the same time that a neighborhood move transformed the universe by offering "The Macarena."

Granada's Sacromonte area, only north of the celebrated Alhambra fortification and only east of the Moorish quarter of Albayzín, is home to the city's flourishing Roma (Vagabond) people group.

Both the English word "Rover" and its Spanish partner, gitano, originate from "Egypt" — where Europeans used to think these roaming individuals had started. Today, as we've come to comprehend that "Rovers" really originated from India — and as the expression "Tramp" has procured negative implications — the favored term is "Roma," since "Vagabond" has gained negative undertones.

Subsequent to moving from India in the fourteenth century, the Roma individuals settled generally in the Muslim-involved terrains in southern Europe, (for example, the Balkan Promontory, at that point constrained by the Footrest Turks). Under the medieval Muslims, the Roma delighted in relative resistance, and acknowledged for their long legacy of craftsmanship and aptitude with raising creatures and blacksmithing.

The main Roma landed in Granada in the fifteenth century — and they've stayed tight-weave from that point onward. Today 50,000 Roma call Granada home, a significant number of them in the area called Sacromonte. In the greater part of Spain, Roma are more absorbed into the overall public, however Sacromonte is a huge, unmistakable Roma people group.

Numerous Spaniards, including some who view themselves as tolerant and hostile to bigot, guarantee that in keeping up such a tight network, the Roma isolate themselves. The Roma call Spaniards payos (whites). Ongoing blending of Roma and payos has brought forth the term gallipavo (chicken duck), in spite of the fact that's who relies on whom you inquire.

While the neighboring Albayzín neighborhood is a rambling zone covering a ridge, Sacromonte is a lot littler — exceptionally conservative and soak. Most houses are tunneled into the mass of a precipice. These moderate, down to earth cavern residences — warm in the winter and cool in the mid year — are likely what attracted such a large number of Roma to the slope.

Sacromonte has only one central avenue: Camino del Sacromonte, which is fixed with caverns prepared for voyagers and cafés prepared to battle about the bill. (Try not to come here hoping to get it on anything.) Interesting paths keep running above and underneath this primary drag — a lofty climb above Camino del Sacromonte is the precipice hanging, parallel optional road, Vereda de Enmedio, which is less touristy, with a really private vibe.

In a progression of whitewashed surrenders along a peak edge, the Cavern Exhibition hall of Sacromonte, otherwise called the Middle for the Understanding of Sacromonte, is a sort of Roma outdoors society gallery about Granada's remarkable Roma cavern staying convention (however it doesn't have much on the individuals themselves). As of late as the 1950s, this complex was as yet a clamoring network of Roma cavern occupants. Presentations feature the local living space of the slope, neighborhood Roma specialties, and let you see a normal cavern home and kitchen — while getting a charge out of awesome perspectives to the Alhambra.

The historical center is somewhat of a trudge to get to, however it's beneficial in the event that you can join your encounter with one of its mid-year flamenco and additionally old style guitar shows. Flamenco has a long convention in Granada, and the Roma of Sacromonte are credited with building up the city's one of a kind of the Andalusian artistic expression — making this historical center, with its magnificently beautiful setting, an especially fine scene.

Sacromonte is a decent spot to see zambra, a flamenco variety where the vocalist likewise moves. About six cavern bars offering evening zambra sessions line Sacromonte's principle drag; two settled zambra settings are Zambra Cueva del Rocío and María la Canastera. Encountering flamenco in a Roma cavern resembles seeing craftsmanship in situ — another open door for an exceptional involvement in this hypnotizing city.

Dusk is here, and I found myself at a spot to be in Granada — the amazing San Nicolás perspective disregarding the fortification of the Alhambra. At this place, at the city's outlandish Moorish quarter's edge, darlings, widows, and vacationers jar for the best perspective on the slope topping, floodlit fortification, the last fortress of the Spanish Moorish kingdom. For more than seventy decades, Spain, the country that is highly dominated by the Catholics, Spain, were governed under the leadership of the Islam guideline, up to the year 1492 when the land was retaken by the Christians.

As of today, Granada is a superb blend of the two of its Christian and Muslim past. It boasts a Profound South experience — a casual sensation that appears to be common of once amazing spots, which has gone beyond prime. As the night comes in, the network turns out and praises life on welcoming and stately squares. Canines sway their tails to the beat of present day nonconformists and road artists.

Granada's predominant fascination, the Alhambra, catches the district's background of triumph and reconnect: its animal Alcazaba post and tower, the expand Palacios Nazaries, the redesigned nurseries of the Charles and Generalife V's Royal residence, which is the Christian Renaissance load worked in a "So there!" signal once the Reconquista came to an end. That is what is overcoming human advancements do: fabricate their royal residence on their adversary's royal residence. The Alhambra is rated as the top sights in Europe, however numerous voyagers never get the chance to see it since tickets are usually sold out. Sagacious explorers make an early booking.

Moorish brilliance bloomed in the Alhambra. Their visual culture was flawless, cunningly consolidating structure and feel. Rooms are embellished through and through with cut wooden roofs, scalloped stucco, designed artistic tiles, filigree windows, and hues aplenty. What's more, water, water all over the place. So uncommon and valuable in the vast majority of the Islamic states, the most perfect image of life to the Fields is none other than water. The Alhambra is improved with water: stopping, falling, concealing mystery discussions, and dribble dropping energetically.

Muslims abstain from making pictures of living animals — that is God's work. Be that as it may, Arabic calligraphy, for the most part lyrics and refrains of applause from the Qur'an, is all over the place. One expression — "just God is successful" — is rehashed multiple times all through the Alhambra.

At the point when Christian powers restored their standard here in 1492, their triumph gave the establishment to Spain's Brilliant Age. Inside an age, Spain's the best, Charles V, became the most influential man on the planet.

The Illustrious Church is the leading Christina sight, and the last resting spot of Ruler Isabella and Lord Ferdinand, who ruled during the last reconnect. At the point when these two wedded, they consolidated their colossal Castile and Aragon kingdoms, establishing what ended up present day Spain. What's more, with this amazing new domain, Spanish eminence had the option to fund numerous extraordinary voyagers. Columbus lopsided his plan to Lord Isabel and Lord Ferdinand to fund a long ocean journey to the "Orient" in Granada.

Granada's previous center, the Alcaicería, is close to the house of prayer and was, at one time loaded up with valuable merchandise — salt, silver, flavors, and silk. Secured inside 10 invigorated doors, it's a sham today, however this brilliant work of shopping paths and overrated knickknacks is as yet amusing to investigate.

The city's old Moorish quarter, the uneven Albayzín, has comfortable teahouses, elegant yards, and complex back streets where you can feel the Middle Easterner legacy that pervades such a large amount of the locale. As of today, close to one million Muslims are in Spain, and that incorporates almost 10% of Granada's occupants. Yet, Fields are not the main culture that has left its imprint here.

About 50,000 Roma individuals ("Rovers") live in Grenada. You'll see some Roma ladies meandering the boulevards pushing sprigs of rosemary at visitors — don't look or acknowledge a twig, or they will be able to bug you for five Euros for a "tip." Roman artists provide energetic night appears in the uneven locale of Sacromonte, engaging vacationers bearing nice guitar plucking and some moves, like flamenco. The cozy shows are done in the surrenders that were the initial residence of the Granada's Roma people group.

There is a familiar axiom: "Give him a coin, lady, for there is nothing more regrettable in this life than to be visually impaired in Granada." There is quite a lot to see in the city, yet it uncovers itself in erratic manners. It will take a writer to deal with and amass the muddled fragments of Granada. Friend via the mind boggling cross section of a Moorish window. Feel the sound of the burbling water inconspicuous among the labyrinth of fences at the Generalife gardens. Tune in to a woodwind vibrating somewhere down in the twirl of rear entryways around the church. Try not to be visually impaired in Granada — open every one of your faculties.

In spite of European travel's whole lifetime, there is still a universe of firsts. As of late, for instance, I had my first involvement with venery.

While at Ireland's School of Falconry (only outside of Cong, north of Galway), an incredible guide grabbed our visit bunch on a "peddle stroll." For about 60 minutes, we meandered through the captivating Ashford Stronghold grounds, with our guide donning a Harris sell on his lower arm. In the wake of finding out about falconry, every individual in our gathering got a chance to hurl and catch a flying creature on his or her arm. With each hurl, the gage was pivoted to the following individual and the guide took care of some little chicken meat the cushioned palm — and the bird of prey realized exactly where to return. The experience was both cozy and exceptional.

All through Europe, you can discover clear and noteworthy creature exhibitions and encounters. They run the range, from celebrated celebrations (Spain's Running of the Bulls or Siena's Palio steed race) to routine ceremonies (sheep shearing or pooch bolstering). Regardless of whether huge and rambunctious or little and personal, I generally discover these encounters entrancing.

The aristocrat who still lives in Château de Cheverny, in France's Loire Valley, is a functioning tracker, and keeps around 70 dogs nearby. The pet hotel is the area of an exceptional nourishing free for all every day at 11:30 a.m. — a fun display that displays the mutts' severe preparing.

As encouraging time nears, the dogs — half English foxhound and half French Poitevin — get stirred up realizing that red meat is en route. The coach corrals the mutts and spreads out the entire dining experience. They're nourished once in a single day, so the fervor is tangible. The coach at that point opens the door and keeps up control as the mutts, who can possibly eat when the mentor gives the thumbs up, assemble energetically around the nourishment. It's an activity in charge. At last, he shows the sign... and it's chow time.

In Vienna, a social feature is watching the Lipizzaner stallions perform at the glorious Spanish Riding School. These magnificent white steeds are a making of Habsburg Archduke Charles. He had obtained the Andalusian ponies from Habsburg-ruled Spain and afterward mated them with a nearby line. They are popular for their respectable stride and florid profile.

A particular Sunday morning, I chose to visit one of their exhibitions in the chandeliered Rococo riding corridor at the core of the city, neighboring the terrific royal Hofburg castle. I parted with close to €25 for a standing-room spot (the seats are priced considerably more — to an extreme, to my brain) just to be there as the much-cherished stallions make their dance moves to well pieced jolly Viennese old style music.

Similarly noteworthy is the steed appears at the Regal Andalusian School of Equestrian Workmanship in Jerez, Spain. Here, steeds — both thoroughbred Spanish ponies and bigger blended breeds — play out an equestrian artful dance with movement, simply Spanish music, and outfits from the nineteenth century. The strict riders then direct their capable, and submissive steeds to dance, hop, bounce on their rear legs, and do-si-do so as to the music.

As I welcome the class and magnificence of a pony appear, I likewise love the natural straightforwardness and closeness of a sheepdog exhibit.

At Kissane Sheep Homestead, a 2,500-section of land ranch roosted on a picturesque incline over Ireland's Dark Valley (close Killarney). The family of John Kissane has been raising sheep for 5 ages. Guests get the chance to visit with the family and find out about their business, and after that watch exceptionally hung sheepdogs race around as indicated by John's call. On my latest visit, one of the siblings disclosed to me — while sheep shearing with much ease — that, since the Irish fleece industry is so terrible nowadays, their ranch endures just gratitude to the cash produced by flaunting the convention to visiting vacationers. (While they typically do exhibitions only for visit gatherings, free explorers are free to be part a booked demo — simply call way in advance.)

What's more, at Leault Working Sheepdogs close Inverness, Scotland; twelve upbeat fringe collies appear to excite to flaunt their aptitudes to guests. The shepherd here starts with a short chat on the foundation of taking care of sheep, at that point exhibits how he directions his anxious collies. Observing each pooch react with exactness to various directions of whistles and yells is amazing. On this homestead, it was extremely clear: Sheepdogs are keen — and sheep are morons.

The best creature shows are fascinating and instructive, yet in addition strikingly genuine and socially expanding — giving bits of knowledge into ages old conventions and various lifestyles.

Once, while going during the 1970s, the young inn where I had intended to remain was full, and the staff guided me to a close by religious circle. As I strolled there, I thought about whether I was marking myself up for exorbitant curfews, straightforward facilities, and Mass at first light.

Without assets for any other thing, I was surrendered. In any case, I shouldn't have stressed — it ended up being a lovely, heartily inviting, and profoundly soothing knowledge. Truly, it was grave contrasted with any lodging, however it had all that I required, was wonderfully spotless, and didn't require to such an extent as a bedside petition.

Around Europe, especially in Spain and Italy, religious circles give peaceful and regularly affordable resting quarters. They can likewise be an approach to take advantage of a profoundly imbued social legacy. Before, numerous well-off Europeans sent a girl or two to a religious circle to live with nuns, where they exceeded expectations at embroidery and heating — abilities still rehearsed today. Currently, medium-term visitors can even now experience life as a Clean sister in Rome, invest some energy in a peaceful religious community nursery, or get a few treats from a sequestered pious devotee in Spain.

To discover religious circle facilities, attempt an aggregator, for example, Cloister Stays or Paradores of Spain. St. Patrick's Congregation in Rome, home to the Catholic American People group of Rome, additionally records puts all through Italy. Nowadays some religious requests have outsiders maintained their guesthouses as organizations, yet there are a lot of communities where cordiality is under the care of the nuns. .

At Casa di Santa Clause Brigida in Rome, for instance, the nuns are five-star-bore has. This sumptuous 20-room community — with a library, rooftop nursery, and magnificent entryways rather than entryways — makes exhaust-recolored sightseers appear as if they have ve passed on and gone to paradise. With mild-mannered sisters floating down cleaned foyers, it's a cool place in dry, medieval Rome — however it's not as efficient as most religious circle stays (about $230 every night).

Numerous religious circles offer just twin beds, and English can be hard to find. Facilities can feel prohibitive to those used to inns; registration hours can be constrained, and a portion of these spots do implement curfews (state, around 11:30 p.m.). You'll have to book most far ahead of time and regard the guidelines of the house.

In any case, the benefits of remaining in these serene spots can more than compensate for the disadvantages. Many are extraordinary arrangements in astonishing areas. In a number of most Catholic urban areas, an amazing religious administrator's castle — truly claimed by the congregation — remains close to the house of God. These days, these previous castles can be perfect spots to go through the night. For instance, directly over Assisi's celebrated Basilica of St. Clare is St. Anthony's Visitor House, where the Franciscan Sisters of the Penance offer a tranquil greeting inside the old city dividers only a couple of minutes' stroll from the primary piazza.

Religious communities can have awesome vibe. You may move into bed in your straightforward room beside a 500-year-old fresco checking on the whitewash on the divider — at that point wake toward the beginning of the day to the sweet pitch of sisters singing songs during Mass. Communities regularly highlight walled gardens — marvelous desert gardens with peaceful, devoted environment, where visitors are allowed to meander and rest.

To sustain your sweet tooth alongside your spirit, search for pious devotee prepared baked goods — particularly normal in Spain. In Ávila, neighborhood nuns make cakes called yemas — delicate, bubbled, sugared and cooled egg yolks; and then sell them all over town.

Arcos de la Frontera, one of Andalucía's white slope towns, has only one outstanding religious circle still in activity. Here, the sisters are sequestered from the general population behind no-"nunsense", spiky window grilles with little peepholes in the latticework to make the nuns see through. Guests venturing into the entryway locate a single direction reflect and a turning cabinet that conceals the nuns from view. On solicitation, one of the sisters will turn out some containers of great, naturally heated nut-studded treats or cupcakes. (In spite of the fact that these nuns don't communicate in English, they have aced Google Interpret.)

For a considerable length of time, the majority of Toledo's almond-fruity-sweet mazapán was made at nearby religious communities — yet with the city's populace of nuns lessening, it's turned out to be hard to get this treat straightforwardly from the source. Luckily, region religious circles still take the mazapán to El Bistro de las Monjas, a cake and café. For a sweet and sentimental night minute, lift some up and head down to the Court del Ayuntamiento, where you can snack your treats on a seat before Spain's most attractive city corridor while respecting the nation's most great church building — worked back when Toledo was Spain's capital — sparkling brilliantly against the dark night sky.

In the case of remaining medium-term, getting a charge out of a tranquil religious circle nursery, or enjoying a sample of

22

sugary gifts from grinning nuns, an European cloister may infuse a quiet vitality into your movements.

With moderately little nations and awesome open transportation, it's anything but difficult to toss a difference in landscape and culture.

Here are a portion of my preferred universal day trips:

London to Paris

Speeding on the projectile train moving from London to Paris (or the other way around), in a passage far beneath the English Channel (the "Chunnel"), is energizing — and just takes about 2.5 hours. Get an early train, go through around ten hours in the City of Light, and be back by sleep time.

This adventure between two of Europe's most noteworthy urban areas is nearly as fun as the goal. At 190 mph, the train is quick to the point that when the tracks are parallel the thruway, the autos look as though they are stopping.

Dubrovnik to Mostar

While numerous voyagers come to Croatia for Dubrovnik and the seaside islands, for me, an excursion inland to Mostar, Bosnia-Herzegovina), is perhaps the most extravagant experience. Paying a visit to these two bits of the previous Yugoslavia resembles changing a history and legislative issues reading material back to front, shaking its substance everywhere throughout the earth. Mostar is a take from Dubrovnik (three hours via vehicle), however definitely justified even despite the outing: Contract a driver, lease a vehicle, or join a trip.

During the twentieth century, Catholic Croats, Universal Serbs, and Muslim Bosniaks, all received a charge out of a genuinely accommodating blending of societies, occupied Mostar. Their disparities were emblematically crossed by a four hundred -year-old, Turkish-tradition stone extension. In any case, as Yugoslavia disentangled in the mid 1990s, Mostar turned into a symbol of the Bosnian War, battled among those equivalent people groups. Barraged by (Croat Catholic) mounted guns shells from the peak over, the scaffold crumbled into the stream.

By 2004, the scaffold had been reconstructed and the city started to flourish once more. Looking over the town from the peak of the extension is an incredible encounter. The cityscape is an image of Mostar's past religious clash. Minarets penetrate the city's horizon like pleased shout focuses, while the chime tower of the Catholic church takes off over them. On the peak above town stands a strong cross, denoting the spot from where Croat powers shelled the Bosniak side of the waterway.

Investigating Mostar is an enjoyment. The city's Hassock impact is clear, from customary Turkish-style houses (counting a few open to guests), to vivacious Coppersmiths' Road (with the kind of a Turkish bazaar), to the call to supplication, resounding all through the city 5 times each day.

Helsinki to Tallinn

An excursion between the capital urban areas of Finland and Estonia gives a Baltic turns to a Nordic agenda. Tallinn is only a two-hour pontoon ride from Helsinki, yet socially it's far off. While Helsinki is progressively current — a tidy and-stone wonderland of shocking nineteenth to 21st-century engineering — Tallinn is cobbled and interesting, with an Old World feeling and the best-protected medieval focus of northern Europe's capitals.

An amazingly unblemished divider encompasses Tallinn's walkable Old Town, partitioned into upper and lower towns. On a one-day visit, investigate the Old Town's cobblestone paths, cabled houses, memorable places of worship, and Fundamental Square, with a cancan of vivid old structures and touristy diners.

For astonishing perspectives, head up to Toompea, the upper town, where you can climb a portion of the first divider towers and visit the Russian Customary basilica. It's an excellent structure, however most Estonians don't care for this congregation, as it was worked to confront the Estonian parliament building and unmistakably intended to utilize Russian social muscles during a time of Estonian national restoration. It's only one of the numerous layers that constitutes up Tallinn as a captivating goal.

Tarifa to Tangier

For me, the most energizing day trip in Europe is to... Africa. From the southern Spanish town of Tarifa, it's only 35 minutes by pontoon to Tangier, offering a real taste of North Africa and a bona fide cut of Islam. While guided trips make things simple, I discover them brimming with buzzwords, from tummy artists to wind charmers. I favor taking the pontoon all alone, and procuring a nearby manual for a meeting at the port.

Tangier is a dining experience for the faculties. The old town (medina) is a twisty chaos of limited ventured paths, impasse rear entryways, and neighborhood life spilling into the avenues. Meander the brilliant produce advertise (souk); look at the workshops of different craftsman's, from mosaic tile makers to tailors; and taste a mint tea on the little square called "Petit Socco" — a similar spot that drew Jack Kerouac and his Beat Age amigos.

As of late, I remained at the edge of the Excellent Socco — the clamoring square between the old town and the new town —

appreciating this well-off, fruitful, serene Islamic city, simply carrying on with its life how it would have preferred to, effectively. It was an excellent minute — and a token of how outskirt jumping can make new encounters and points of view.

At any time my movement ambitions float off to Spain, they regularly incorporate dreams of the southern piece of the nation that appears more consummately Spanish than maybe anyplace else. With a series of camouflaged slope towns, bright skies, and energetic celebrations, Andalucía is the Spain's spirit— characteristically so.

Most voyagers hit Andalucía's 3 incredible urban communities — Cordoba, Granada, and Sevilla — or other nearby areas. In any case, for anything increasingly real, I prefer investigating the area's inside alongside the Course of the White Slope Towns. The medium size towns that spot this undulating course are more open and friendlier than the enormous urban communities; yet at the same time pack a whallop of superbly unadulterated Spanish culture. In the case of squatting in a gorge or roosted on a slope, every town — painted in color white to remain nice in burning summers — possess a character and its very own account.

Investigating these slope towns is most straightforward via vehicle, with just the significant towns effectively open-by-open transportation: train through Ronda and Arcos de la Frontera (via transport).

My most loved is Arcos de la Frontera, a picture taker's blowout. Arcos covers its ridge, tumbling to the ground such as a wedding dress' train. The fantasy traditional focus is an overly complex wonderland, which is a place where you can perspective jump entirely all over the place and enjoy the breeze channel via the limited avenues as autos inch all through the corners. Around town, I like to look tactfully into private yards. These magnificent, cool-tiled patios, loaded up with pools, plants and glad family exercises. These are just normal to the whole area.

Arcos' fundamental church — and the name of the town, as it signifies "on the outskirts"— act as the tokens of the Reconquista, several hundreds of years long battle to deliver Spain over from the colony known as Muslim Fields. Once the Christian powers recaptured Arcos, its main mosque was crushed, which made the congregation was based on its vestiges. As of today, these slope towns — are not vital anymore— are simply sitting back calmly.

A short drive from Arcos will directly take you to Ronda, where almost 35,000 individuals dwell. As a matter of fact, it is the most considerable and engaging command post on the course.

Ronda's principle attractions are its crevasse spreading over scaffolds, a charming old town, and perhaps the most established sports theatre in Spain (worked in 1785). The field's segments corral the activity, making a sort of Neoclassical Theater. Be that as it may, the genuine happiness depends in investigating the back avenues of Ronda and partaking in its delightful overhangs, nurseries, as well as all-encompassing perspectives. Strolling the lanes, you sense a solid nearby network and pride where everybody appears to get introduced to everybody.

While swarmed with all-day stumbling travelers from the close by Costa del Sol, as they day comes to an end, local people recover their squares and lanes, as well as flourishing the dominates of the tapas scenes.

Ronda's stunning roost over a profound chasm, while outwardly sensational today, was pragmatic and imperative at the time it was assembled. For the Fields, it gave an intense bastion, which was the last one that the Spaniards vanquished in the year 1485. The gorge separates Ronda into the traditional old town, as well as the moderately current new town that was worked after the reconquest. The 2 main towns were then associated by an extension in the close of the 1700s.

The emotional street connecting Ronda and Arcosslices via the Sierra de Grazalema Regular Park, popular all through Spain for the rich and rough hilly landscape. Inside the recreation center untruth the two towns of Grazalema and Zahara de la Sierra. Whereas Grazalema is the a medium-term stop of the two, the other town, Zahara is a pleasure for the individuals who need to feel just the hints of the breeze, winged animals, and old strides on antiquated cobbles.

Modest Zahara has an awesome view above the turquoise store. The town had for some time been a key fortification for the Fields, as well as Spanish Reconquista powers thought of it as the portal to Granada. As of today, the château is minimal in excess of a suggestive destruction with a telling perspective.

Grazalema is also one of the prettiest town, offering an imperial overhang for a vital excursion, a good place for those who want to watch old-clocks battling the game of cards, and a lot of peaceful, whitewashed avenues to investigate. Shops merchandise lovely high quality fleece covers and great quality calfskin things from close by Ubrique. Whereas the Sierra de Grazalema Common Park is popularly recognized as the spot with most rains in Spain, the mists appear to squeeze themselves out before they arrive at the place.

In any of these towns, the prime time is always the evenings. The leisure starts as everybody inclines toward the focal square. The feet of families licking frozen yogurt clean the perfect avenues daily. The entire town walks — it resembles "cruising" without vehicles. Purchase a frozen yogurt, join the procession, and absorb the pith of Spanish life.

The quintessential picture of Spain is the southern locale of Andalucía, which is known for bullfights, whitewashed slope towns, and stylish Mediterranean hotels. Also keeping in mind that a significant part of the area's intrigue is in its slope and beach front retreats, at the core of Andalucía lies 3 extraordinary urban communities: Sevilla, Cordoba, and Granada.

Granada is the celebrated Fields' final home, or the Muslim, as it is called, who were led out of Spain before coming back to Africa somewhere towards the end of 1492 at the time of Reconquista — the "reconquering" of Spain by Christians and Spaniards. Alhambra is its leading sight, the last and most prominent Moorish royal residence in Europe. Roosted on a slope and loaded up with beautiful luxurious scalloped filigree windows, stucco, percolating wellsprings, and quiet pools, the royal residence features the quality of Moorish progress in the thirteenth and fourteenth hundreds of years.

While quite a bit of Granada feels Spanish, the Albayzín — the old Moorish quarter — holds its complex, Moroccan-souk feel. Situated on a slope opposite the Alhambra, it has dazzling perspectives crosswise over to the castle. I prefer to be here at dusk and have my meals at one of the view eateries or outing at the San Nicolás porch, which accompanies incredible Roma (Rover) music about throughout the day. Pop a couple of cash into the performers' cap, and appreciate an outside show on a par with numerous you may pay substantially more for.

On account of its centrality in the Reconquista, Ferdinand and Isabel, the best lord and ruler of Spain, chose to utilize Granada as the main capital. It was at this place, which they tuned in to the final pitch of Christopher Columbus for an ocean voyage to the main Orient and consented to fund the excursion. Imperial House of prayer hosts the explorers who want to see the ruler and rulers intricately cut Renaissance-style gravesites.

Cordoba is around a hundred miles northwest of Granada, another extraordinary city of Moorish, which also as well as the Mezquita, an awesome previous mosque. When the core of social capital of the western Islam, the Mezquita has got rid of some of its magnificence after some time — making it simple for guests to envision the feeling of Islamic Córdoba in its prime of tenth century. Within the main mosque, an enormous sixteenth century church ascends from the middle. At the point when the Christians appeared, rather than decimating the main mosque, they constructed their congregation in it.

Despite the fact that a few voyagers pause in Córdoba for only a couple of hours to rush the nearby city, it merits going through some hours to be able to investigate different parts of the city: the main Jewish quarter, with a little yet wonderfully saved synagogue; and the pride of the city— its yards. The brilliant small edens fill in as open air living areas, holing up behind mind boggling ironwork entryways and loaded up with blooms flooding in the midst of beautiful pottery and entryways.

Whereas Granada boasts of the incomparable Cordoba and Alhambra has the surprising Mezquita, Sevilla has a spirit.

Sevilla's two major sights are its house of prayer and illustrious castle. Not at all like in Córdoba, Reconquista Christians tore down the mosque of the Sevilla to construct a house of God, reporting their goal to enable it be so enormous that "any individual who sees it will take us for psychos." Today it's as yet the second-biggest church in Europe (by volume), after St. Dwindle's at the Vatican.

Only a couple of remainders of the previous mosque remain, including the goliath ringer tower, which was before the minaret. Today, guests can winding up the slope to the highest point of the chime tower for amazing perspectives. The basilica likewise hosts the tomb of Christopher Columbus' that is being lifted up by a total of 4 rulers.

Sevilla's old royal residence (Alcázar) is brightened with a blend of Christian and Islamic components — a style known as

Mudejar. Whereas the Alhambra in Granada was worked by Fields for their respective leaders, Sevilla's Alcázar was worked by Moorish craftsman in the style of Moorish, generally for Christian rulers. Marvelously embellished corridors and patios have unmistakable Islamic-style thrives; for example, expound structures on stucco, bright earthenware tile, lobed curves on thin segments, and Arabic composition on the dividers.

The royal residence is likewise where Ruler Isabel managed the matter of the nation's nautical investigations. In the Chief of naval operations' Corridor, Columbus related his movements and Magellan arranged for him a trip to the globe. Today, displays call up the period of Columbus and Spain's New World predominance.

Each time you decide to pay Sevilla a visit, flamenco is an unquestionable requirement. This music-and-move work of art has its underlying foundations in the Roma and Moorish societies. The men do the vast majority of the ostentatious automatic weapon footwork while the ladies regularly focus on agile turns and smooth, rearranging steps. In the rough voiced howls of the vocalists, you'll hear echoes of the Muslim call to petition. Exhibitions run from genuine shows to traveler driven shows to off the cuff late-night sessions at easygoing bars — yet even the touristy shows are rich with heartfelt quality.

Southern Spain's three major urban communities give an intriguing take a gander at the Moorish impact on the culture of Spain. Each merits a visit for knowledge into this one of a kind corner of Europe.

Dining in Europe is all about something other than the nourishment. The best eating encounters are tactile, where you are not just consuming scrumptious cooking; you're additionally getting a charge out of the glaze of age, the vivid demographic and their prattle, and the embrit sound of blades slicing via the newly heated portions of bread. Following quite a while of movement, I've discovered that similarly as significant as historical centers and holy places is encountering society through the kitchen, hearth, as well as the lounge area table.

To get an important dinner, there is no need of taking your meals at a spot that bears the Michelin star, hold up in a long queue, or utilize a given travel site like to disclose to you the kind of foods you can easily find. You only need a couple of honest proposals on the venue the local people eat — simply inquire from a retailer or an hotelier.

You will locate the highest legitimate feasting spots enjoy a little determination on a written by hand menu jotted in local dialect. The menu is little since they will concoct exactly all that they are able to merchandise out for the afternoon, it's written by hand since it's molded by whatever's crisp sold at that particular moment, and it happens to be in one language since they're focusing on neighborhood, and the return clients as opposed to vacationers. Toward the night's end, you might be lucky to have a culinary specialist join your team, who needs to thrive in the fun and good times the individuals are enjoying a direct result of his cooking.

An incredible spot to eat with local people is at a market corridor, for example, Kleinmarkthalle in Frankfurt; Torvehallerne KBH in Copenhagen; or Mercato Centrale in Florence. All across the European continent, Modern Age steel-and-glass ranchers markets are obtaining yet another rent on life as in vogue nourishment corridors. Regardless they accompany the ranchers' market measurement, yet they have been spiced up with incredible diners, evaluated for nearby customers and serving some of the freshest fixings. The same number of is intended for the working group, they will in general be most lively at noon. To pick a slowdown, search for a line of local craft persons: They drink and merry —make each day and perpetually recognize the best spot for a reasonable chomp.

I am not a party time mixed drink sort of a person, yet in European continent, I prefer to slow down from the touring day with munchies as well as hard drinks out on the town square. At night, at bars all through Europe, understudies and carefree individuals are out having their spritz. In spite of the fact that you for the most part need to abstain from eating at these spots, I joyfully pay an excessive amount to appreciate some espresso or a mixed drink on the most costly bit of land nearby and watch the scene pass by. Consider it leasing a spot to have fun.

It is a common knowledge that in quite a bit of Europe, brilliant eaters are able to recognize the area and month judging on the content on the menu at a decent café. I will in general request day-by-day specials, which typically feature what's regular (or I take a gander at what local people are eating). For example, a plant known as white tall plant from the lily family, can be used to heal the sense of taste in spring... however leaves the cooler the remainder of the year. In the event that the soup of French onion and cheddar-melted cheese are found on the menu in summer, the spot is a sham — a café for local people will not be comfortable serve its customers these winter dishes in a month such as July.

I additionally make it a point to attempt territorial claims to fame, for example, cassoulet in the southwestern part of France, the Segovia's broil pig or the fiorentina in Florence (produced using the Chianina (white) type of dairy cattle munching all through Tuscany). Portugal's Barnacles are costly, yet so justified, despite all the trouble — the best fish that I have eaten at any point eaten.

At whatever point conceivable, I request family style hence I can be in a position to eat my way through a greater amount of the menu. In some cases, instead of obtaining 2 principle courses, my movement accomplice and I share some bit of smorgasbord of canapés or initial courses — they are filling, more affordable, and more regularly nearby than dishes. These little plates pass by various names all through Europe.

If there is any of the ceremony that I prefer after a serious dinner then it is to move to my inn and enjoy the tranquil scenery of a town during the evening. A few times, I've recognized a gourmet expert kept in a seat out of his café, tasting some wine or alcohol and seven smoking.

Based on my personal review, a critical European dinner is an all-encompassing background. It is climbing twenty minutes to a Greek shoreline and looking over a presentation instance of plates arranged within the industry fixings and the top catch bought straightforwardly from the anglers, or devouring the 3 hours on an out and out Italian supper with numerous courses and unending glasses of alcohol, at that point visiting the gourmet specialist when the supper surge closes. It is everything part of the eating culture in Europe, and what makes travel here so exceptional.

On warm Spanish evenings, bars are loaded up with revelers who wash down starter estimated bits called tapas with pitchers of fruity sangria.

Sangria is a refreshing summer drink. Brilliant red in shading, it takes its name from the Spanish word sangre, which signifies "blood." The key fixings are red wine and natural product. It's frequently spiked with something more grounded to give it a kick. Schnaps, gin, and vodka are normal added substances, however you can utilize anything you desire or happen to have inside arm's scope.

Each bar or café has its own adaptable formula. Sangria's fruitiness can make it taste misleadingly innocuous until your head begins to turn. Pace yourself cautiously until you've decided the amount of a punch it packs.

In case you're making sangria at home, there's no correct method to do it. Some portion of its magnificence is you can make it as intense or manageable as you like. You can even make nonalcoholic sangria, substituting natural product juice and soft drink water for the wine.

To make the alcoholic kind, start with a jug of red wine. A full-bodied Spanish red, for example, a rioja is ideal. You can utilize whatever organic products you like. Apples, pears, peaches, grapes, and berries are generally prevalent. (Cut huge organic products like apples and pears into little pieces. Be certain littler organic products like grapes and cherries are seedless.) Citrus natural products, for example, oranges and lemons are especially great on the grounds that the sharpness tempers the sweetness. Include soft drink water — and a couple of sprinkles of hard alcohol in the event that you like. Improve it with sugar and chill it with ice.

Sangria specialists state the pitcher ought to sit for a few hours before you drink it so the organic product absorbs the liquor. Regardless of whether you're in Toledo, Spain, or Toledo, Ohio, on a sweltering summer day, sangria is an invigorating drink that offers some relief from the mid-year heat.

¡Salud!

Markets with an energy for ham and pickles, bullfights in nice bars blasting on the television, secluded nuns merchandising cupcakes, the towns in Spain — regardless of whether renowned among sightseers or obscure — accompany a lot of approaches to interface with the culture in the neighborhood.

In the only southern city of Sevilla however; I might have been any place in the country. Its engaging business sector is the very initial stop in the whole journey. The fruit lady urges me to attempt wart is referred to as anderilla, which got its name due to the troubled skewer, which a bullfighter places into the bull. While I cautiously place an onion from the small stick of salted carrots, and olives, she instructs me to consume it at that instance— what could be compared to tossing off a fix of vodka? The woman around the nearby meat slow down blasts into chuckling at my stun.

Just in the same manner pickles do, the meat slow down — or salchicheria — is a significant piece of any market in Spain. In this country, as far back as Roman occasions, December is always the time for butchering the pigs. Once that has been done, they are dried after salting each conceivable piece into different hotdogs, hams, and pork items. By pre-summer, the meat, which is now salty is relieved, ready to persevere the warmth, and then hung in enticing business sector shows. Ham thankfulness is enormous here. While in Spain, I am a devotee.

As yet making the most of my tests, I would always be on the move, and in a cool dim bar loaded up with extremely old, and short folks. Any Spanish man who is over a particular age had their entire development spurt years attempting to endure the fierce Common War that ran for about four years. The individuals who performed, for the most part did so marginally. That age is very short as compared to the individuals of the following.

Around the bar, the representation — is glued on the television, viewing the last game of a long arrangement of the bullfights. Nearly everyone in the family of El Cordobés is in the fight.

Wondering about at the fun at the bar and modest rundown of hard beverages and wines, I request a Cuba Libre for about 2 dollars. The beverage is prepared firm and also tall, with some peanuts in a dish. All of a sudden the whole place wheezes. I'm not able to accept the striking screens. The pack thunders as El Cordobés covers used his arms to cover his head as the bull stomps on and attempts to gut him. TV always rehashes the scene ordinarily.

El Cordobés endures and — nothing unexpected — in the long run slaughters the bull. As he makes a triumph lap, grabbing bundles hurled by worshiping their fans, and the camera would just emphasize in on the tear uncovering his hip and a 10"-long wicked injury. The male who I always hang around will recall and discussion about this minute for a considerable length of time.

At the cloister, found devoutly on the following corner, nobody takes note. The windows are always open with substantial spikes and bars as though to shield the isolated religious women from the rage of the bull bar. Flying in the faintly lit anteroom, I press the signal and the squeaky lethargic Susan turns, uncovering a pack of crisply prepared cupcakes and macaroons. I purchase cupcakes to help the charity project of the religious community. Having a feeling that Tom, I'm able to observe — even if it is not-exactly single direction reflect — the sister in her streaming attire and propensity immediately show up and vanish.

Sparing my hunger for supper, I donate the cupcakes to kids as I meander on. My city walk finishes at a different religious community — that is currently the best café around the local area, Restaurante El Convento. The glad proprietor, María Moreno, clarifies the menu. As chapel chimes thump, she discharges me a full glass of some delicious red wine.

Requesting for the best ham, I received a plate of the delicious jamón ibérico. Maria clarifies that, whereas very costly, it is just top of the line, from oak seed sustained pigs with dark feet. It really improves, a bundle of its personal and a nice delayed flavor impression.

I disclose to Maria the male at the following table appears like El Cordobés. A single look and she utters the following words - "El Cordobés is significantly more attractive." By the time I notice his ongoing dramatization, she adds, "It's been a troublesome year for bullfighters."

Chapter 2: Oh My!

Conceived in Spain, the child of a craftsmanship educator, the teenaged Picasso immediately progressed past his instructors. He aced camera-eye authenticity yet in addition demonstrated a compassion for the individuals he painted that was astute past his years. As an adolescent in Barcelona, he fell in with a bohemian group that blended wine, ladies, and craftsmanship.

In 1900, Picasso set out to positively influence Paris, the undisputed world capital of culture. He dismissed the surname his dad had given him (Ruiz) and picked his mom's rather, making it his particular single word brand: Picasso.

The reckless Spaniard rapidly turned into a poor, yearning to go home outsider, engrossing the styles of numerous painters while looking for his own craftsman's voice. He discovered friendship among individual monstrosities and pariahs on butte Montmartre. At the point when his closest companion ended it all, Picasso dove into a "Blue Period," painting starved poor people, hard-peered toward pimps, and himself, packaged facing the cold, with eyes all shouted out.

Picasso's Ladies

Ladies were Picasso's fundamental subject. As a craftsman, he utilized ladies both as models and as dreams. Having intercourse with his model enabled him to paint the lady's physical highlights as well as the enthusiastic relationship of their relationship. At any rate that is the thing that he told his better half.

In the present psychobabble, Picasso was a vain and harsh male, a sex fiend energized by his own weaknesses and powerlessness to associate personally with ladies.

In the language of Picasso's group — saturated with the analysis of Freud and Jung — relations with ladies enabled him to express basic desires, recoup stifled recollections, go up against his association with his mom, find shrouded facts, interface with his anima (female side), and reproduce the prototype encounters lived since the get-go.

After around 1910, Picasso never painted (just outlined) from a presented model. His "representations" of ladies were frequently composites of a few unique ladies from his enormous index of recollections, sifted through passionate affiliations.

In the same way as other voyagers, the previous spring I went to Barcelona longing to check out Antoni Gaudí's amazing Sagrada Família church. By the time I arrived, they had already shut the ticket office, with this particular sign: "No more tickets today. Purchase your ticket for one more day on the web." Fortunately, I'd known to book tickets ahead of time.

Alongside Sagrada Família, Spain's sights to book in advance and incorporate Barcelona's Picasso Historical center, and the Imperial Alcazar Moorish royal residence, Church of the Friend in need, and house of prayer in Sevilla. Royal residence of Catalan Music, and Cadaqués all demand a pre-organized visit, which additionally should be reserved ahead. Sold tickets for the Dalí Theater-Historical center in close by the city of Figueres are additionally a smart thought. Whereas it might be in fact conceivable to purchase tickets nearby, in my manuals I basically state you should save ahead of time. It's a lot more astute.

Barcelona keeps on developing. After a long redesign, the Oceanic Exhibition hall has revived, showing thirteenth to eighteenth century ships (reclamation proceeds on the later-century ships). The area of El Raval is ascending as the new sector for bohemian. Whereas this region has unpleasant edges, its as of late revived Sant Antoni showcase lobby, new Historical center of Contemporary Craftsmanship, and walker neighborly avenues add to its blast of innovative bars, shops and cafés.

In northern Basque nation of Spain, San Sebastián's initial tobacco industrial facility has seen various transformations over into the free Tabakalera Worldwide Community for Contemporary Culture, facilitating movies and workmanship displays — and knockout perspectives from its rooftop porch.

In Pamplona, another show gives an in the background take a gander at the town's popular bullring.

In the south of Spain, the church in Sevilla presently runs housetop visits, giving a superior view — and experience — than its chime tower climb. In close by Córdoba, you would now be able to climb the chime tower at the Mezquita, the enormous mosque-turned-house of God. Be that as it may, Córdoba's fourteenth century synagogue is shut for remodel.

Spain's system of transportation is likewise improving: Uber is currently accessible in both Barcelona and Madrid. Madrid's Metro has another battery-powered card framework: A red Multi Card (tarjeta) is required to purchase either a solitary ride Metro ticket or 10-ride travel ticket. Spain's rapid Alvia train presently keeps running among Segovia and Salamanca in around 75 minutes, making it quicker than driving.

Portugal has less blockbuster sights than Spain and not even close to the groups. The main sight where you may have a group issue is the Religious community of Jéronimos at Belém, simply outside Lisbon legitimate (purchase a combo-ticket at Belém's Paleohistory Exhibition hall to keep away from the ticket line at the cloister).

Riding in a large portion of Lisbon's exemplary trolley vehicles — a quintessential Portuguese encounter — can likewise be frustratingly packed (and tormented by pickpockets focusing on visitors). A less-swarmed choice is trolley line #24E — which is back in administration following a decades-in length rest. In spite of the fact that this course does not really pass many top sights, you will be able to see a cut of workaday Lisbon. (Or then again, even better, get your trolley involvement in Porto, which has no groups.)

On my last visit I understood that Lisbon's cherished Alfama quarter — its Visigothic origin and once-salty mariners' quarter — is salty no more (aside from with the perspiration of journey gatherings climbing its now-inert paths). The new brilliant zone to investigate is the close by Mouraria, the memorable tangled quarter on the posterior of the manor. This is the place the Fields lived after the Reconquista (when Christian powers retook the city from the Muslims). Right up 'til today, it's a dirty and beautiful locale of outsiders — yet do not postpone your visit, as it's beginning to improve simply such as the Alfama has.

In other Lisbon news, the Historical center of Old Craftsmanship completed its highest floor redesign, and plans to remodel its 2nd floor in 2020. One of the city's driving cafés, Pap'Açôrda, has moved to the principal floor in the Ribeira advertise corridor (a.k.a. the Break Market). It is still suggested and as yet serving customary Portuguese cooking.

In the journey town of Fátima, where the Virgin Mary is rumored to show up in 1917, the new Fáti María Moreno ma Light and Harmony Display kept running by the Roman Catholic Church supplements a special walk to the basilica, and provides a more satisfying knowledge than its increasingly business rivals.

In Coimbra, ticket alternatives for the College of Coimbra sights, with the lovely Ornate Lord João library included, presently spread the close by and noteworthy Science Exhibition hall — go there first to purchase your college tickets and book your required coordinated passage for the library.

In Porto, the Bolhão Market is shut for a genuinely necessary redesign until mid-2020. Meanwhile, merchants are in the storm cellar of a close by retail establishment... carrying on the warm customer connections that return ages.

Portugal and Spain have a ceaselessly advancing touring scene, so it' is imperative to go in 2019 with the most recent data to capitalize on your experience.

Tucked into a twist of its waterway, the Andalusian town of Córdoba has a radiant Moorish past. While its old divider inspires the historical backdrop of a sometime in the past domain, its rich cityscape and jovial squares demonstrate a cutting edge pride. Run of the mill of southern Spain, it's a human inviting spot loaded up with vitality and shading.

Córdoba's focal point is its enormous previous mosque — or, in Spanish, Mezquita (for articulation ease, think female mosquito). Supernatural in its loftiness, this tremendous structure overwhelms the willy nilly old town that encompasses it. At its apex, in the tenth century, the mosque was the focal point of Western Islam and a social center that matched Baghdad and Constantinople. A miracle of the medieval world, the mosque is astoundingly well-safeguarded, allowing guests to acknowledge Islamic Córdoba and the wonder long stretches of Muslim standard.

Terrific entryways lead to an open air patio protected by orange trees. Sometime in the past, admirers washed here before petition, as coordinated by Muslim law. Entering the mosque, you step into an incredible backwoods of sensitive sections and effortless curves that appears to subside into vastness, as though mirroring the giganticness and multifaceted nature of God's creation.

Inside, it's anything but difficult to picture Córdoba as the focal point of a flourishing and modern culture. During the Dim Ages, when quite a bit of Europe was boorish and ignorant, Córdoba was a sanctuary of edified idea — celebrated for a noteworthy soul of religious resistance, aesthetic articulation, and commitment to theory and technical disciplines. Jews, Christians, and Muslims had made sense of how to live respectively pretty much agreeably. Everybody communicated in a similar language, cooked similar dishes, wore a similar sort of garments, and had a similar open showers. It was one culture, with three religious customs.

Be that as it may, in 1236, when Christians vanquished the city, everything changed. As indicated by legend, one morning Muslims said their last supplications in the extraordinary mosque, and that evening the Christians set up a versatile special stepped area to commend their first Mass. Afterward, as though planting a cross into the mosque's religious heart, they assemble an overwhelming house of God in the Mezquita. Transcending overhead, the house of God's ringer tower encases what had been a minaret. In its juxtaposition of customs, the Mezquita exceptionally epitomizes the interaction of Spain's Christian and Muslim societies.

Córdoba has a stronghold (Alcázar), a fourteenth century synagogue, a Roman extension, and the (shamelessly professional Muslim) Exhibition hall of Al-Andalus Life, yet most travelers leave the city having seen just the Mezquita and the knickknack shops and adorable medieval quarter that encompass it.

Córdoba is significantly more than its verifiable self. A short stroll past the vacationer zone takes you to a crisscross of private paths, whitewashed and slender. Individuals truly live here. There are no crude shops, and pretty much the main visitor is... you.

Go on a forager chase for yards. For a break from the hot, dry atmosphere, local people retreat to outside porches to chill. These generally concealed spaces are normally tucked behind luxurious ironwork entryways. As you meander, look into any open porch entryway to get a look at a fancy retreat (property holders are glad to flaunt their yards).

Blooms are up front in Córdoba each May, when the city commends a progression of celebration occasions. First comes the Skirmish of the Blooms march, with ladies hurling blooms from bloom secured buoys to excited groups.

Next, for the Celebration of the Crosses, neighborhoods gladly make and show ten-foot crosses decorated with blossoms. Occupants assemble for a considerable length of time in advance to set up their crosses covertly; in a prior time, the work gatherings were a reason for youthful singles to meet. Maybe the most symbolic Córdoba occasion, nonetheless, is the Porch Rivalry, when inhabitants open their nurseries to people in general in an extraordinary challenge to choose to the city's most alluring yard. In the event that you have an affinity for yards, visit the Palacio de Viana (a.k.a. the Yard Historical center) to walk its 12 associating porches, each with an alternate subject.

Córdoba is a simple day trip (it's a short train ride from Sevilla) — however on the off chance that you truly need to know the spot, go through the night. Like wherever in southern Spain, evening is prime time. All through the spring celebration season, local people pack the squares in network wide festivals. During the Celebration of the Crosses, every local affiliation sets up a bar beside its blossomed cross to serve beverages and tapas (the nearby forte is salmorejo, a smooth rendition of gazpacho). Smooth guitar notes and enticing flamenco beats fill the air.

Encountering the conventional culture of Córdoba — celebrated by and for its local people — bests any bundled vacationer appear. With its wonderful yards, energetic conventions, and irresistible environment, Córdoba rewards the individuals who aren't in a rush.

To encounter a more relaxed town and an opportunity to day-outing from the Europe to Morrocco, let Tarifa be your preferred command post. Spain's (and Europe's) southernmost port is a charming Bedouin looking town with an exquisite sea shore, an old manor, eateries swimming in new fish, reasonable spots to rest, and enough windsurfers to sink a ship.

You can visit Tarifa's tapas bars for delicious tidbits, enjoy a spectacular whale-watching journey, or simply kick back before your hurricane trip over the Waterway of Gibraltar to Africa. Tarifa has no blockbuster locates (and is tranquil in winter), however it's where it just feels great to be in the midst of a get-away.

A visit to St. Matthew, the town's primary church, offers a look into Tarifa's history. A minor square of an old Christian headstone implanted in one of the congregation dividers (dated Walk 30, 674) demonstrates there was a working church at the times of Visigothic, before the Moorish success. A few years after the fact came the congregation's "entryway of exonerations," going back to the late fifteenth century, at a time when Tarifa was on the edge of the Reconquista. During the period when the Spain's Catholic Rulers were driving the Fields back to Africa, Tarifa was a perilous spot. To urge individuals to live here, the Congregation offered a tremendous measure of pardoning to any individual who stuck it out for a year. One year and one day subsequent to moving to Tarifa, they would enjoy the benefit of going through this exceptional "entryway of absolutions," and a thanksgiving mass would be held in that individual's respect. These days, in the night times, it appears life squirts from the congregation out the front entryway and into the carefree central avenue, fixed with bistros and bars.

For fine perspectives on the harbor, move to the Manor of Guzmán el Bueno's base. The manor, today just a solid mass, obtained his name from a thirteenth century Christian general who picked up notoriety in a tragic demonstration of fearlessness while battling the Fields. Holding Guzmán's child prisoner, the Fields requested he give up the manor or they'd slaughter the kid. Guzmán can't, notwithstanding tossing his own blade down from the bulwarks. It was utilized on his child's throat. At last, the Fields pulled back to Africa and Guzmán was a saint. Bueno.

Tarifa has a sub-par rate bullring where learners mess up battles on periodic Saturdays through the mid-year. Proficient bullfights occur the main seven-day stretch of September. There are blurbs all over the place, and you will be able to see them.

On the off chance that you want to watch creatures in their characteristic territories, a few organizations offer whale-and dolphin-watching journeys. For any of the visits, it's savvy to hold one to three days ahead of time, however same-day appointments are conceivable. You will receive a multilingual visit as well as a 2-hour trip. Note that sightings happen more often than not. Pilot whales and the dolphins skip here all over the year, whereas the sperm whales visit May through July and orcas remain in the two months of July and August. Contingent upon the breeze and climate, vessels could decide to come from Algeciras rather. The drivers will always follow a professional guide they are assigned.

The immense, sandy sea shore Playa Punta Paloma lies around five miles northwest of town. On breezy summer days, the ocean is covered with run windsurfers as the seashore holds close to 100 fun-mobiles and vans coming from the northern Europe. Under mountain edges fixed with current vitality producing windmills, it's an intriguing scene. Move through the sandy street and walk around the sea shore. You'll discover a cabana kind of villa with rental rigging, beachwear shops, a bar, and an eatery or two. For drivers, it's a snap to reach. In the absence of a vehicle, you're in karma July through the month of August, when reasonable transports do a circuit of close by the campgrounds, which are all on the waterfront.

Day Outing from Spain to Morocco

Tangier, in my view, is the fundamental motivation to go to Tarifa. The quick current sailboat ride (an enormous vehicle ship that speeds over at regular intervals throughout the entire year) takes not exactly 60 minutes. You stroll from the Tangier port into a surprising city — the 5th-biggest in Morocco — which is never again the Tijuana of Africa, however a blasting town getting a charge out of the energetic help as well as a can-do vision of the Moroccan lord.

Most vacationers do the thoughtless hip twirling and-shopping outing. They are then met by a guide, taken on a transport visit and a stroll in the old town showcase, given two or three coarse Kodak minutes with desert artists and snake charmers, and offered lunch with unrecorded music and hip twirling. At that point they visit a major shop before being led down to their pontoon where —about 5 hours after they landed — they come back to the Main World appreciative they do not have looseness of the bowels.

The option is to just take the ship without anyone else and leave the traveler track. Things are modest and moderately sheltered. Since in excess of 90 percent of guests pick the solace of a visit, autonomous swashbucklers once in a while observe another vacationer and stay away from all the traveler kitsch.

You can get the principal pontoon (9:00) and spend the whole day, restoring that night; stretch out with a medium-term in Tangier; or even head further into Morocco (you'll need another person's manual for that).

Meandering the Craftsmanship Deco avenues of Córdoba in southern Spain, I'm attracted to a disturbance on a square. It's nearly 12 PM — everybody's out, enjoying a cool night. Short men with rough tobacco-husked voices and enormous guts — called satisfaction bends— bump and bark as twelve little school young ladies clatter an improvised stage... taking a shot at their sultry. Indeed, even with iPods, mobile phones, and straight teeth, the culture of Andalucía's flamenco still endures.

Córdoba — the number-three city in Andalucía (after Granada and Sevilla) for touring — is visited generally for its Mezquita — a tremendous mosque with a house of God worked in its center. That Mezquita, one of the wonders of Moorish Spain, is encompassed by a touristy zone of shops and visit bunch well-disposed eateries. Past that, there are no groups. What's more, late during the evening there are less travelers yet.

Keeping away from vacationer groups is significant nowadays — particularly when making a trip in pinnacle season to prominent goals like Córdoba. If it's all the same to you take you meals late and the smoke, cheerful local people encompass you uniquely. I've seen that in Spain, an eatery prescribed in every one of the manuals may have some feelings of a sham — loaded up with Americans — at 8 or 9 o'clock. Be that as it may, by 11 p.m., the vacationers head for their inns and local people retake their turf. All of a sudden "touristy" eateries are loaded up with enthusiastic cafes — all nearby. I've additionally seen that a few restaurateurs are satisfied to have their best eating zone be the smoking zone — the proposed outcome: a solid neighborhood following...with not many sightseers. Any voyager willing to overcome the smoke (which isn't that terrible) will do well here.

Furthermore, as anyplace, simply meandering the back boulevards gets all of only you with the town. Investigating the private back paths of old Córdoba you can get a reminiscent whiff of the old town before the ongoing opulence hit. As you investigate, be a sharp spectator.

Lanes are restricted — intended to give much refreshing shade. To keep things much cooler, dividers are whitewashed and thick — giving a sort of regular cooling. To counter the exhausting whitewash, entryways and windows are brilliant. Iron flame broils spread the windows. Generally these were progressively imaginative, presently increasingly down to earth — a token of the diligent hole through the ages among rich and poor. Stone guards on corners secured structures against rash drivers. As you'll see, rummaged used antiquated Roman columns functioned admirably. Paths are built using stream stone cobbles: modest and nearby. They gave depletes down the center of a path as they were flanked by smooth stones, which remained dry for strolling. Leftovers of old towers from minarets endure, incorporated with the present structures. Muslim Córdoba crested in the tenth century with an expected 400,000 individuals... and loads of now-for the most part, past neighborhood mosques.

Yards in Cordoba are paid attention to very. That is particularly clear each May when a savagely aggressive challenge is held to pick the city's generally pleasant. Yards, a typical element of houses all through Andalucía, have a long history here. For instance, the Romans utilized them to chill, and the Fields included lavish, beautifying contacts. The porch worked as a calm open air family room, a desert spring from the warmth. Inside expand ironwork entryways, roses, geraniums, and jasmine spill down whitewashed dividers, while wellsprings play and confined feathered creatures sing. A few yards are possessed by people, some are collective patios for a few homes, and some effortlessness open structures like historical centers or communities.

Today, mortgage holders invest wholeheartedly in these smaller than expected heavens, and have no issue offering them to visitors. Look out for square metal signs that demonstrate memorable homes. As you walk Córdoba's back avenues, pop your head into any wooden entryway that is open. The proprietors (who keep their inward dark iron doors bolted) appreciate flaunting their completely flawless porches. A grouping of Córdoba's past yard challenge grant champs keeps running along Calle San Basilio and Calle Martín Roa, only opposite the Alcázar's nurseries.

Well after 12 PM, my social scrounger chase is finished and the city at last appears to be peaceful. I move into my bed.

Similarly as I portion off, a loud and multigenerational march thunders down the cobbled path that I thought guaranteed a decent night's rest. Remaining in my clothing and enveloped by the curtains, I peer cryptically out my window. Underneath a band of guitars and castanets with an ensemble of those rough tobacco voices channels down my tight back street. Grandmas — watchmen of a diligent culture — ensure the youngsters get their Andalusian conventions. I feel like a Peeping Tom... until one lady gazes toward me, gets my attention, and appears to gesture as though fulfilled that I was seeing the tireless extravagance of their customary culture.

The tale of Spain has every one of the rushes, disaster, frenzy and motivation of a Shakespeare type of dramatization — and they are also valid. What's more, in the event that you realize where to direct your glaze, you can peruse this particular history in Spain's extraordinary structures. For a fast "Precipice's Notes" examining, how about we visit four extraordinary sights: Sevilla's church building, Sevilla's Alcázar, the El Escorial royal residence outside the city of Madrid, as well as Barcelona's Gaudi's Park Güell in Barcelona.

Spain's history is ruled by close to seven hundred years of pushing the Muslim Fields (who attacked in 711, assuming control over all of Iberia) once more into Africa. All through Iberia, it appears to be each old church was based upon a mosque. There is no bolder case of this than Sevilla's enormous church building. Envision the wicked battling: Muslim against Christian. At last, with the fight over — Christians remaining among grisly groups of vanquished Fields — the victors took a gander at the tremendous mosque (which was constructed hundreds of years sooner upon a Visagothic church) and announced, "We'll tear this down and assemble a cathedral...so enormous, individuals later on will take a gander at it and proclaim us lunatics." Just the minaret was then kept, redesigned into a ringer tower with colossal lettering on top pronouncing, "This is more grounded now, made for the sake of God." And close to it lingers the greatest Gothic church on the planet. Glance closely around what probably comes to your mind is..."madmen!"

It's no incident that 1492 is a date renowned for two occasions: the last ejection of the Fields, and Columbus' "revelation" of America. Maybe the force of the fruitful Reconquista pushed Spaniards into the Western side of the equator as conquistadors. This no nonsense blend of the globe's most roused pioneers, fortune-trackers, shipbuilders, and Spain's banner that had supposedly been planted by an evangelist, and religion around the world — empowering Spain to beat Britain to the case that the sun didn't manage to set on its domain.

Over the square coming from Sevilla's rambling church building is its rambling Alcázar royal residence, a Christian castle worked in a Moorish style. As Christians conquered back Iberia, numerous Muslim specialists and engineers remained on the landmass, giving a brand new society designed the Mudejar style. (Mudejar implies, actually, "the individuals who remained.")

The Alcázar feels like a Middle Eastern Evenings fantasy: finely scratched vaults, silky arcades, keyhole curves, and comfortable patios. At the middle of this lies the carefully proportioned fourteenth century Court of the Ladies. You will be able to find the architects made a shrewd small-scale atmosphere: water, plants, earthenware, and thick dividers,...all just to be fine. It's a fine case of this Mudejar style. While the stylistic theme is Arabic or Moorish in style, you'll see portrayals of peacocks, creatures, and rulers (which you will not be able to discover in evident Muslim stylistic layout). The dividers are ornamented with an adapted Arabic content. In more established Moorish structures, for example, Granada's Alhambra, this content makes a visual serenade of Koranic sections. Be that as it may, in this particular Christian castle, the Arabic content relates New Confirmation stanzas and publicity phrases, for example, "committed to the heavenly Sultan Subside — because of God!"

Christopher Columbus is enormous in Spain, particularly in Sevilla's Alcázar. It was here that Ruler Isabel questioned Columbus after his New World disclosures... and understood this could be extremely huge economic affair. She later made another royal residence wing to direct Spain's New World endeavors in 1503.

America was not by any means the only thing being found as the fifteenth century thundered into the sixteenth. According to conventionalists, a perilous new age of humanists and Renaissance masterminds appeared to delight in blasphemy (they accepted the earth was round, but was also a long way from the focal point of the universe). It was additionally the age that led to the breaking of the Roman Catholic's imposing business model on Christianity in Western side of Europe. After an extended religious war, the mainland split: half wound up Protestant and half stayed Catholic. Every half accepted the other was in Satan's grasp. Spain, driving the individuals who stayed faithful to Rome, initiated the Counter-Transformation (with Europe's mightiest armed force enhanced by teachers, questioners, and future holy people) to secure and enroll however many spirits as could be expected under the circumstances for its equitable Catholic reason.

A thirty-mile side-trip from the city of Madrid will lead you to the modern-day monumental royal residence, El Escorial. The strict Monasterio de San Lorenzo de El Escorial is a finished reversion from the rich (even sexy) Alcázar. Rather, it radiates a calming blend of intensity and straightforward religion. This sixteenth century combo royal residence/religious community gives us a superior vibe for the Counter-Reorganization and the Investigation than some other structure. Worked when Catholic Spain had a feeling of being undermined by Protestant blasphemers, its development overwhelmed the economy of Spain for an age (1563–1584). In light of this domineering jerk in the national spending plan, Spain does not have anything else to appear from this very dominant time of her history.

The goliath, bleak structure made of dark stone looks more like a jail than a royal residence. The length of around 650 feet and a width of about 500 feet, it has 2,600 windows, 1,200 entryways, in excess of 100 miles of sections, and 1,600 overpowered voyagers. 400 years prior, the puzzling, contemplative, and incredibly Catholic Lord Philip II led his realm and coordinated the Investigation from here, encompassed dividers, well-scoured floors, and grim decorations. Today it's a period container of Spain's developing "Brilliant Age," stuffed with history, workmanship, and Probe phantoms.

El Escorial was brought about by Phillip II as a multi-reason complex, including a great sepulcher for Spain's illustrious family, a religious community for loads of petition for the imperial spirits, a little royal residence to give a sort of Camp David for Spain's eminence, and a school to grasp humanism in a "boundaried" way that likewise advanced the Catholic confidence. In the colossal library it's reasonable: Training was a need for the Spanish eminence. When you opt to exit, you should think back over the entryway. The speckle cautions "Excomunion..." (i.e., you'll be banished in the event that you grab a book but fails to look at it appropriately). Who needs late expenses when you finally get the keys to condemnation?

As we push forward in time, quite a bit of Spain's increasingly present day design feels like a repeat of its past. Be that as it may, Barcelona is an exuberant exemption. As Europe moved from the nineteenth to twentieth century, it praised a rising way of life and almost a century without a noteworthy war. Future unrests were in their initial, starry-peered toward visionary steps. Impersonators left their studios to give the nurseries a new paint, and Craftsmanship Nouveau draftsmen constrained hard steel and cement into milder natural figures. Barcelona's response to Craftsmanship Nouveau was Modernisme, and its virtuoso was Antonio Gaudí.

To value Gaudí's work you have to get it. For example, his beautiful, breathtaking Park Güell sitting above Barcelona was a spot I never loved — until an encounter with a neighborhood direct. Instead of the recreation center it is today, Gaudí initially expected this nursery to be a 60-living arrangement-lodging venture — a sort of gated network. As a high-pay lodging improvement, it slumped. As a recreation center, it's a pleasure for nearby families. Also, similar to the Sagrada

Família church out there, it offers voyagers an interesting look into the erratic character of the planner and his occasions.

Envision if this gated network was loaded up with Barcelona's well off, and you lived there. Venturing past extravagant gatehouses, you'd stroll by Gaudí's fashioned iron gas lights (his father was a metal forger and he generally delighted in this medium). At that point you'd climb the fabulous stairway past the fired mythical serpent wellspring. You might choose to drop by the Lobby of hundred Segments, a produce advertise for the local's 60 manors, while at the top. These fun sections, each unique (produced using concrete and rebar, bested with beautiful pottery, and covered with broken jugs and bric-a-brac), add to the imperativeness of the current market. In the wake of shopping, you would definitely proceed up, looking down along the fun loving "pathway of segments" that help a long arcade. Gaudí drew his motivation from nature, and these curve like a surfer's ideal "tube." At the highest point of the patio, you'd unwind on a bright seat (intended to accommodate your body in an agronomical way) and appreciate probably the best view.

100 years prior, Gaudí's gleaming new Park Güell was not in the right shape— excessively a long way from Barcelona's social scene — and it flopped after only two homestead had been built. Taking into account that the city's wealthiest neighborhoods encompass the recreation center today, it

appears Gaudí's gated network conceptualize was only a century comparatively radical.

Chapter 3: Check Out the Spots

I never feel sick of tapas. Certainly, you can discover them in certain American urban areas, however for purposes of genuine fun of taps, you should visit Spain. It has an encounter that resembles a palatable forager chase, where I gather little parts of fish, servings of mixed greens, meat-filled baked goods, and southern style, and sort them out for just a short night dinner. Tapas are a chance to dine boldly — and a genuine, reasonable approach to test nearby dishes.

Barcelona flaunts incredible "tascas" — bright tapas bars — on Gothic Quarter. In the city of Madrid, an area known as Lavapies provides a multi-ethnic embroidered artwork of Madrileños appreciating pointed, modest, undesirable yet carefree life in the city as well as the bars tapas.

In the Basque Nation, tapas are all the more frequently called the pintxos. Some portion of the experience of Basque is participating in a txiquiteo — jumping from one bar to another, getting a charge out of wine, little open-confronted sandwiches, as well as certain small pepper snacks, nuts and mushrooms. Whereas enticing cold pintxos are consistently in plain view the bars in Basque, and prepared mainly for consumption, I like to request the list containing hot pintxos calientes for anything straight from the kitchen — such as arachnid crab or meat cheeks deeped in a nice wine sauce.

My tapas recollections are striking: In the core of the district of Andalucía, during the typical cool summer times, I elbowed up to a tapas bar in Granada clamoring with gabbing local people. A blackboard menu portrayed different contributions, ham pawns balanced like ox-like ballet dancers seen at the roof, as the Spaniards hung over one another to yell their forthcoming tapa request to the barkeep.

Pursuing down a specific bar almost nullifies the point and soul of tapas — they are off the cuff. To locate the most true tapas environment, I search for uproarious barriers with heaps of nourishment trash on some portion of the tapas convention, bunches of local people, as the television is booming. Mainstream TV review incorporates soccer and bullfights matches, as well as the Spanish understandings of cleansers and senseless show of games. Whereas tapas are always served throughout the day, the genuine activity starts late — 9 p.m. at the most punctual. However, for learners, a previous beginning is simpler and accompanies less upheaval.

When I blitzed tapas bars in Ronda promptly at night with Antonio, a nearby guide and companion. I required some food before going all through that southern Spain slope area to check eateries, yet it was not feasible for the person to arrange any possible thing. Since a number of the Spaniards operate up to 7:30 p.m., a dinner at either 9 or 10 p.m. is commonplace — and Antonio was unable to place his head around the possibility that I might take my meals at 6 or 7 p.m.

Tapas served in a plate would not go past 4 USD. To set aside cash, keep away from fish that can go up to the price of $14. A number of the restaurants tend to push bigger parts called raciones (supper plate-sized) instead of littler tapas size of the saucer. Request the littler tapas partitions, recorded as "½ ración" on a menu, however numerous restaurants do not serve any food littler than just a ración.

Generally, tapas are always consumed remaining at the counter, a place in which it is simpler to blend. I would prefer to just sit, however Spaniards always think that it's progressively regular to remain on their feet to snack — yet they truly prefer to sit when they smoke. Standing bodes well in case you're on a financial limit since nourishment and beverages are generally least expensive served at the barra.

You will have more chances of paying more to be at a plateau (table) and even more for the open-air table, or for a terraza. Find the value list (regularly placed in nice kind on a divider some place) to recognize the choices of menu and value levels.

In any case, a calm bite and take the drink on a patio on the square of the town is definitely justified regardless of the additional charge. Be that as it may, the least expensive spots once in a while receive the favorite show. Remain within the bar and concentrate the barkeep — he's a craftsman.

Be decisive or you will never get the services you are looking for. If you don't mind catches the person's eye. Get a fun, modest sampler plate. Request different minimal open-confronted sandwiches.

Ensure that the feast is undertaking. Request a banderilla, a little stick of zesty, cured veggies — eat it at the same time for the real punch; which obtained its name after the lance bullfighters applied something great at that time. Try some expensive kept ham from oak seed. Crunch on the squid arms, marinated and salty dogfish, or even some snails.

The bars in Tapas are the focal point of the fun at nigh urban areas and towns all over the country. Addition (or simply phony) gratefulness for these great tastes, and you will forever be loved for doing this.

Try not to stress over buying up to the point where you are prepared to leave; the barkeep is monitoring the tab. To receive the bill, request la dolorosa — truly "the trouble"). The joints may accompany a language obstruction, and a little jargon will enable you to eat better, yet you can likewise simply point to things in the showcase case.

For a reasonable and available cut of the culture of Spain, plunge heedlessly into the main adventure. You will be remunerated with reduced down flavor's punches, a sensible bill, and the tenacious vitality of local people that encompass you.

Sevilla, the capital of Spain's southern Andalucía locale, is as profound a spot as I've at any point been. It's an awesome to-be-alive sort of town, where the shade of flamenco dresses, tunes from guitars, snap of castanets, and warmth off the boulevards join into an elating murmur.

The entryway to the New World in the sixteenth century, Sevilla blasted during Spain's Brilliant Age. The voyagers Christopher Columbus, Amerigo Vespucci, and Ferdinand Magellan cruised from its extraordinary stream harbor, finding inexhaustible wellsprings of gold, silver, cocoa, and tobacco. For a period, these New World wealth transformed Sevilla into Spain's biggest and wealthiest city.

The present Sevilla has a lot of amazing sights, including Spain's biggest house of prayer (with the tomb of Columbus) and an incredible Moorish castle and nursery (the Alcázar). Be that as it may, the top thing to encounter here is the murmur of road scenes and the city's one of a kind customs.

Sevilla swings effectively from the sacrosanct to the mainstream. Heavenly Week — between Palm Sunday and Easter — is commended with extraordinary reverential intensity here (book ahead). Throughout eight days and seven evenings, upwards of 100 sparkling pious statues are strutted over the cobblestones at painfully inconvenient times by the devoted.

Be that as it may, with the religious occasion off the beaten path, the disposition movements to party mode. Up to 14 days after Easter, a lot of Sevilla packs into its immense carnival for the April Reasonable. Incalculable tents line the paths, everyone a private gathering zone of a family, club, or affiliation. Consider it seven days of dusk 'til dawn affairs, with the attention on moving, drinking, and mingling.

On opening day, the cream of Sevilla's general public motorcades around the carnival in carriages or on horseback. Men wear customary suits with fitted jeans and a short coat, and women turn out in splendidly hued flamenco dresses.

Since the gathering tents are open just to individuals and their visitors, solicitations are pined for. In case you're not fortunate enough to have a Sevillan companion who can get you in, advance toward one of the seven open tents. The sherry is dry and copious, and the nourishment is fun and modest.

Fortunately, a tent with bunks is accessible for anybody requiring a snooze.

Sevilla is the origination of another sort of gathering: flamenco. It's as yet the best spot to encounter this emotive move and-music type of snapping fingers, stepping feet, and clicking castanets. A considerable lot of the shows around the local area are intended for vacationers, however they are genuine and riveting (and typically a decent worth). On the off chance that you keep awake to the extremely early times, you may be fortunate enough to get a late-night set in an easygoing bar. In these cases, flamenco is a colorful occurring, with onlookers applauding along and empowering the artists with challenges and yells.

Indeed, even nourishment is a showy occasion in this town. The vivid tapas custom got its beginning in Andalucía, and Sevilla is the area's noshing capital. Great, outdated tapas bars are all over, however these days gourmet places, with spiffed-up stylistic themes and imaginative menus, are the wrath. Indeed, even in troublesome monetary occasions, when different organizations are shutting down, these bars are springing up everywhere. Local people clarify that with the breakdown of the development business in Spain, designers, engineers, and different experts — energetic for a business opportunity — are putting resources into new popular bars.

I generally discover some new information when I travel. This time in Sevilla, my tapas guide exhibited how quality jamón (restored ham), cut slim, will adhere to a plate when you overturn it. I don't know what that has to do with quality, yet one thing I am certain of: When in Spain, life's too short to even consider eating fair jamón. At any rate once, pay extra for the best ham on the rundown.

For an alternate curve on tapas, however, search for an abacería, a bygone era market that serves as a tapas bar. The blend isn't totally surprising, the same number of tapas gourmet specialists depend on Spain's excellent canned nourishments in forming their delectable goodies. Press into the back room of one of these spots, and you're crushing back in time. Scouring elbows with neighborhood eaters in an abacería, encompassed by tinned sardines and canned peaches, you'll feel like you're in on a mystery.

To stroll off a dinner on a moderate night, meander into the Barrio Santa Clause Cruz, Sevilla's once-flourishing Jewish quarter. This tasteful labyrinth of paths is unreasonably slim for vehicles however ideal for winding among little squares, tile-secured porches, and whitewashed houses hung in blossoms. Getting lost is simple, and I suggest doing only that. Orange trees flourish, and when they bloom in late-winter (typically Walk), the fragrance is grand.

Rhythms change rapidly in Sevilla, from the force of flamenco's beat to the calm of its back rear entryways. It's road theater that everybody can participate in.

In Spain's Andalucía area, celebration and religiosity go connected at the hip: a similar enthusiasm and vitality devoted to celebrating is placed into long, serious, religious parades which stop up the city's restricted lanes.

I found this when I was taping a scene of my open TV program in one of my preferred cafés in Córdoba. I was working with Isabel, an enchanting neighborhood direct who discussions about nourishment with the enthusiasm of a mother discussing her kids. Each plate appeared to sparkle. The feast was specially made for television: a montage of Spanish joys from the simmered almonds and fiery green olives that hit the table naturally, to the neighborhood salmorejo (like an excessively thick, splendid orange gazpacho), boquerones (anchovies), singed eggplant, and "Middle Easterner Plate of mixed greens" with cod and sensitive orange areas.

The bull-tail stew, or rabo de toro as it is commonly referred appeared as dim as meat can be…almost inky in flavor. The jamón ibérico — a blessing from the eatery — is Spain's best ham and is also over the top expensive. Our bit was sparkling with taste; eating it was what could be compared to sticking a boutonniere onto a tux. The wine was the thoughtful they bring out exceptional glasses for.

Feeling a bit underdressed for the shooting; I got back to a taxi and sped to the inn between courses. In transit, we passed a square flourishing with individuals celebrating. In transit back, a similar road was obstructed by a religious parade; I needed to exit and make my way. One moment I was excited to be in the café shooting such brilliant nourishment; the following I was flabbergasted we were missing gatherings in the squares and a colorful religious parade in the boulevards.

Energized, I asked my two-man television team to film the parade. Seeing liquor filled celebrating around a transcending red cross — trailed by a dismal parade — was impactful and ground-breaking. Everybody races to the roads to be a piece of the religious function. Trumpets boom a ballyhoo, youngsters convey a buoy, and candles bump as one as the marchers float in the corner of the night.

Travel in Andalucía is this way. There are continually some ongoing activities. We then made our way to Córdoba for the Celebration of the Crosses, at a place where every local gatherings around its own transcending cross that is composed up of red carnations. Church chimes make a call to petition, however a call to celebration. Local people eagerly utilize this extraordinary day on the congregation schedule as a springboard for a network party.

The following day, the gatherings were fundamentally finished. We at long last discovered one square around the local area that was energetic. It was the first time they were taking part in the challenge, they had won first prize, and it appeared they'd been celebrating from that point forward. The scene was basically full of hung-over, and depleted joy — as though they'd been eating, drinking, and moving for a whole day (which they likely had). Presently the cross was surrendered — missing carnations just the same manner a bum misses teeth — and the moving was finished. The remainder of the partiers assembled around the temporary bar, which appeared to give physical help to those resolved to continue. I required moving around the cross for our Program. Our guide said they were done moving. Be that as it may, with a straightforward solicitation, I had the option to animate the group, and the yard was indeed flourishing with outstretched flamenco.

We'd been in Andalucía for seven days, and I understood it could be referred to as a hair-trigger flamenco society. I usually prefer hair-trigger societies. Similarly as Austria is a hair-trigger dancing society, Andalucía is simply trusting that the least complex reason will place castanets into movement and move.

On that Córdoba's little court, I admonished the depleted pack to move just next to their drained carnation cross. Inside seconds the vitality and enchantment of the earlier night's gathering had reignited. Crooked arms, conditioned legs, heels with disposition, streaming hair...everything agitated with a smooth Andalusian soul. Like crickets shaking their wings in a mating custom, Andalusian ladies — wearing their peacock delicacy — clicked their castanets.

With enough moving recorded, I let the phony party bite the dust, and everybody continued their positions — opened doors by the bar. They filled a jug top with a custom firewater shot and offered it to me. As 2 dozen spectators watched, I brought down it. With my head tossed back, realizing that the camera had stated rolling and every single Andalusian eye were on me, I was dove into what appeared to be a long quietness. I needed to state something extremely cunning or important. Be that as it may, I could just think of a buzzword — "Olé!" No issue. Everybody cheered.

I'd for the longest time been itching to attend a soccer game... civility of a neighborhood hotelier whom we had changed pleasantries while in the city of Rome. The match set the main group Roma up against the group of Florence, or the Florentina as they were called.

Joining on the arena, Stefano left on a control (tipping two or three hooligans to watch — or possibly just not destroy — his vehicle). I found the square around the soccer arena in Roma; it's encompassed by Mussolini-time's main statuses, in the asphalt as yet proclaiming his self-imposed title "il Duce" ("the Pioneer").

The arena alone has been completely upgraded, and it is no big surprise. Soccer is Italy's top game — all things considered in the vast majority of Europe. Headliners are paid millions and given the treatment of leading movie stars. Little children wherever are brought up professing to score the triumphant objective simply prefer them. On major game evenings, bars and brew nurseries are stuffed with the fans gathered around Televisions. After a misfortune, they suffocate their distresses. After a triumph, they merry make by passing through the city avenues sounding horns and waving group banners.

As a result of this energy, things can gain out of power. There were not kidding occurrences of hooliganism and revolting during the 1980s and 1990s — in Italy as well as over the landmass. Be that as it may, when I went, authorities had gotten serious about football fan brutality, and genuine advancement was made at getting control over the raucousness.

As it appeared to be, it was an agreeable game I found in Rome. Be that as it may, the soul in the arena was humorously dastardly. At American school football match-ups, each time a particular player is playing, quietness lies on the stands as players kneel down to implore. In Italy, when somebody's harmed, the rival group's fans serenade, and "Devi morire!" "You should pass on! You should kick the bucket!"

The region past the objective is constantly loaded up with the modest seats intended for the most ardent fans — they stand and sing the whole time, waving immense banners and hurling sparklers that sound like a gun discharging. At the game I visited, the amplifier checked on the different budgetary, criminal, and group punishments that accompany fierce activities and supremacist and prohibited trademarks.

Stewards encompassed the little unforeseen of Florence fans like an uproar squad. Once the game was done, they remained in their seats while the Rome fans withdrew. At that point the Florentines were accompanied securely to their anticipating transports to get back home (for this situation, tragic after a 1-0 misfortune).

In case you're going in Italy — or anyplace in Europe — the best thing to do would be to break out of the traveler mode and feel just like they are close to the door at a coordinate of the soccer. Everybody, paying little respect to age or social class, is a specialist, speedy with a supposition on a mentor's lousy choice or a ref's amateurish lead. Fans usually prefer to affront authorities: An Italian most loved is "arbitro cornuto" — "the official is a cuckold"; every nation has its very own one of a kind put-downs.

In the event that you are attending any game played in the Europe, you will have to pay a premium to be able to watch groups in the top proficient associations, for example, Britain's Head Class or Italy's Serie A. In any case, in the event that you opt to watch the lesser groups in the lower divisions, you will typically get a seat.

In the event that you do not possess energy for the soccer coordinate, think about paying a visit to a soccer arena. In Britain, numerous groups offer reasonable, well-run arena visits — check your preferred group's legitimate site for subtleties. If by any chance you are planning to go to Barcelona, think of a journey to Camp Nou, one the best groups in expert soccer. A visit brings you into the pressroom, by the container seats, via the room of the trophy, and even past the warm-up seat, finishing in a same-level perspective on the field. You'll additionally get the chance to visit an exhibition hall following the features of the history of Barca, for example, the six title cups the group won in a solitary season — an accomplishment, they state, that will never be rehashed.

Soccer fever warms up in Europe for significant competitions like the quadrennial European Titles (a.k.a. the Euro Cup) and World Cup. Search for colossal television screens at significant parks and squares as local people assemble the give a shout out to the home group.

Regardless of whether you could be in Europe during a title or at the standard the season, thud yourself down in a bar, bistro, lager nursery, or sports bar and request that a fan clarify their national fixation. Numerous Europeans put their national, provincial, and individual pride on their competitors' backs. It's a buzzword that remaining parts valid: In an Europe settled, the soccer field is always the battleground.

Europe's most noteworthy real urban areas are loaded up with energizing clamor and exciting "I've for the longest time been itching to see this" sights. Yet, the glory of a major city can get overwhelmed rapidly by the commotion of humankind and the panicky strain to pack in the touring. Joyfully, Europe's urban areas all offer serene stops and gardens to walk, bicycle, or simply sit and human watch.

Here are a couple of my preferred spaces in three occupied urban communities to make tracks in an opposite direction from the groups, slow down, and hear myself think while I take in the nearby scene.

Paris

On my latest summer excursion to Paris, the exceptional vitality of Paris' riverside esplanade along the Seine got me stuck. This is a space offered over to enjoy a luxurious lifestyle. In what used to be a road occupied with traffic is another world for working out, messing around with the children,

What's more, for a month each mid year, a single mile stretch of the Seine's Correct Bank transforms into the Paris Plages — beautiful urban sea shores with several sand in plenty. It is this string of whimsical fake sea shores that has pruned palm trees, loungers, and parlor seats, and not the Reviera River. That makes it a fun unwinding zone. You'll likewise discover "sea shore bistros," climbing dividers, a nice library, prefab pools, sea shore badminton, volleyball, as well as Frisbee zones.

Somewhere else in Paris, everyday citizens always abound just as the privileged people do because of the parks: Tuileries Nursery is the most amazing park at the city was at one time the place of lords and rulers. It has remained a superb spot to set free your brain in the wake of survey such work of art. Dissipated among these greenery beds are a few bistros, lakes with toy vessels for lease, and trampolines for hopping.

Luxembourg Nursery is one of the most delightful places in Paris. It's occupied yet at the same time unwinding; probably the prettiest (and calmest) segments lie around its edge. Inside its 60 sections of land, lies a serenity and a cool precision, with extraordinary principles administering its utilization (for instance, nice for playing the cards, and mutts can be strolled. It is also a nice place for the jokers. Move to a green seat pondside, go running, or enjoy some tennis or b-ball, or look for one among the many games that you can play while there. The splendid, flawlessly cared blossom beds are totally checked for three occasions in a year. May is the time when the boxed trees are taken out of the main orangeries.

Increasingly off Paris' the most common way to go is the Promenade Plantée. Apart from being thin, the park, which has a length of two miles, is a tight nursery stroll on a previous raised railroad line. It's currently a great spot for an invigorating walk or run, and beginner botanists value the changing vegetation.

London

The parks in this city — like pretty much all that is found within the city — sit on an establishment of history. The enticing green surrounding, where rulers used to relax, are presently the grounds where the ordinary citizens can enjoy the sunshine. In the western part of the city is Hyde Park. Having changed its previous name, it's the ideal spot for those who want to play and run free; it's loaded up with lavish green environment— alongside a lakeside pool, paddleboats and bicycles for renting. There is also a court for those who might want to play tennis there. Sundays are great days here, especially from around late morning. The Speaker's Corner at Hyde Park is the place to visit. You will hear a wide range of enthusiastic spirits cause a ruckus about goings-on — and hecklers with contradicting perspectives.

Nearby Hyde Park, lovely Kensington Nurseries was at one time the private play area for Kensington royal residents. It is optimal for walking, around commemorations; wellsprings, statues (counting a bronze Diminish Skillet), and a Subside Dish play territory for the children.

Kew Nurseries is in the western part of London, with three hundred sections of land and over 30,000 sorts of plants. For a speedy visit, you can opt to meander through 3 main structures in the region - a winding current nursery developing endless desert plants, bug-crunching meat eating plants, and that's only the tip of the iceberg known as the Princess of Grains Center, Waterlilly House, as well as the Palm House.

Barcelona

This is the 2nd greatest city in Spain, and is a packed traveler haven — yet you will still discover rest in the nice environment that it has— Fortification Park — a desert garden of nice ways, nice grass and trees, as well as a zoo. Initially the recreation center became the site of the highly despised military stronghold, an Spanish guideline image over the widely-known Catalunya. The city of Barcelona changed the fortification for an All-inclusive Show in the year 1888. The Triumphal Curve, which was at the highest point of the main recreation center filled in as the reasonable primary passageway — emblematically commending the stronghold's expulsion. Appreciate a fancy wellspring, which the youthful Antoni Gaudí, the highly acclaimed Innovator designer in the city, assisted configuration; think about a side trip in a rental paddle boat on a lake.

In some cases the locals pack a lot into their schedules. Backing off to value a recreation center opens you up to a more slow paced, all the more privately grounded way to deal with an outside culture.

As an explorer, I wind up paying a visit to the homes of bunches of demised individuals. Most of them move graceful reflection (William Wordsworth's Bird Bungalow in Britain's Lake Region).

A significant number of my top choices are the home studios of specialists — painters, stone workers, journalists, architects, writers. There is something in particular about these unique places that summons the weird enchantment of imaginative work. Fortunately for voyagers, many have moved toward becoming historical centers that invite guests.

Maybe Claude Monet's is the most prominent of the home studios in Europe. Monet went through forty years developing his nursery and his craft at Giverny, fifty miles in Paris' northwestern region.

The real sky-lit studio is presently a blessing shop, yet the craftsman's genuine shop was his five-section of land garden. An ace of shading, Monet handled his nursery like great treasures, picking and placing his peonies, lavender shrubs, and irises for most extreme impact. Thus, the bloom beds propelled a portion of his most notorious works of art. Walking the way here resembles seeing an painting of impressionist spring up.

The idea of the craftsman's studio got it's beginning when the set up experts kept up workmanship workshops and instructed disciples. At the point when Florence's city fathers began building another house of God in the late 1200s, they established the Show del Duomo, when the figures for the congregation and its ringer tower were made (drama is the Italian word for "work").

Amazingly, the "drama" proceeds with today inside strides of the milestone church building, on the fittingly named By means of dello Studio. Through the open entryway, you can see the present experts chiseling substitution statues and updating old ones to keep the house of God's specialty in decent shape.

After some time, the regular studio turned out to be not of a highly shared workshop, increasingly a position of single market and the reflection. The most prominent author in Norway, Edvard Grieg, kept up simply such an exemplary retreat for the craftsman. His final 22 summers were spent at this place, up to early 1900, at a place he named Troldhaugen, simply a step from Bergen. Calm, rich, and detached, the fantastic spot was perfect for absorbing uplifting fjord magnificence.

Be that as it may, the house was frequently overflowing with companions and close family. To check the steady commotion, Grieg constructed a straightforward, 1-room studio at the edge of the water; consistently he'd lock himself inside to be certain he'd complete some errands. The lodge possessed all that he required: an upstanding piano, a work area disregarding the water, as well as a love seat for snoozes. Looking at the provincial work area, the little instrument, as well as the emotional fjord view from the window, it will be easy see the manner in which Grieg's type of musical tunes so capably inspires the Norway's normal miracle.

Craftsmen from as far back as the Rococo period had made sense of that the studio could serve as a business room. At the point when Rembrandt's profession moved to the Brilliant Age Amsterdam. After moving to a place with a nice studio, he would spend most of his time painting his renowned Night Watch at this place. He also did a number of perfect works of art.

The craftsman fixed the dividers floor-to-roof with his works of art, and afterward welcomed potential benefactors in to peruse. Opening up the studio ended up being useful for business, to such an extent that Rembrandt additionally had a little office to stay aware of his administrative work. (He wasn't awfully great at it, and in the long run failed.) On the off chance that you visit his reproduced house today, you can perceive how he utilized its rooms to show workmanship to potential purchasers.

Maybe the most unordinary home-based painting studio that I have had a privilege of visiting is Salvador Dalí's place just a simple day trip from Barcelona. Dalí enjoyed summers in this languid port town, and the capricious craftsman returned years after the fact with his significant other, Occasion. Together, they assembled a twisted exacerbate that moves up a slope sitting above the Mediterranean.

In the same manner to the specialty of Dali, his house is unique, and enjoyable. The whimsical feel, all around, was ideal for a Surrealist spending time with his inventive mate and dream. This spot, and his organization with Occasion, turned out to be so essential to Dalí, that he opted to stay away forever after he passed on in the year 1989.

From that point forward, everything in their home has been kept pretty much as they left it, from energetically squishy toys and mustachioed depictions to the couple's phallic-molded pool, the area of orgiastic gatherings. In Dalí's studio, with its huge windows drinking in light from the ocean and sky, he painted for eight hours every day (he had cunningly enhanced an easel that could be raised and brought down so he could remaining situated while painting). Dalí lived enormous, however he buckled down, as well.

Regardless of the fact that you could be enjoying a dream in Dalí-land or drifting peacefully over Monet's water lilies, an excursion to a craftsman's home studio can be a critical feature to all of Europe's cities.

It is not so easy to top Spain's most cosmopolitan and fun city, Barcelona. I cherish the spot, and there are so many who have the same feeling. Consistently, 10 million guests plunge into town, meandering aimlessly the Ramblas, visiting shrouded the Old City's corners, and wondering about energetic Modernista engineering.

On the off chance that you need a break from the groups, a multi-day trips from the great city of Barcelona are enticing sceneries: the peak religious community of Montserrat, the Salvador Dalí exhibition hall at Figueres, and the shoreline Cadaqués towns, and the Sitges (extraordinary sea shores).

For very nearly a thousand years, Benedictine priests have lived on Montserrat — the "serrated mountain" —, which significantly comes from the valley floor located in the northwestern part of Barcelona. Writers guarantee that little heavenly attendants cut the mountain with brilliant saws. In any case, with its interesting rock developments and emotional bluff-sticking cloister, this is an intriguing trip for pioneers with (or without) climbing boots. A train ride will just take one hour from. You can also choose to commute with a vehicle, and you will be on the other side within the shortest time ever. Genuine pioneers stroll up.

According to the professionals in this game, in medieval occasions, shepherd kids first saw the lights before hearing melodies originating from the mountain. They followed the action to a cavern, where they came across a statue named "La Moreneta" — "the Dark Madonna." The religious community rapidly turned into a pioneer magnet. The little wooden Mary is right behind defensive glass in the Montserrat basilica, yet the regal circle she supports in her grasp is uncovered, prepared to get the loving pinch of the unwavering. Love birds specifically look for this present Mary's favoring.

For explorers and nature darlings, a funicular trips almost a thousand feet over the cloister. At the peak of the mountain, the air is new and the perspectives are dynamite, clearing (on the most clear days) from the Mediterranean Sea to a place known as Pyrenees. From the trailhead here that is seen in this place, well-signposted climbs transmit out. The most well-known one is generally downhill on your way to the cloister. Climbing along the tranquil trail gives me a feeling of turning cartwheels.

In case you're a Dalí aficionado, make your way to Figueres (two hours north of Barcelona) and the weird, whimsical Dalí Theater-Historical center. From the train station that is located at Figueres, it's a simple 15-minute stroll to the gallery. You can't afford to miss it: with its pink colors, covered with brilliant portions of bread, and beat with and a geodesic vault and stupendous eggs. For aficionados of Surrealism and Dalí, it's one of Europe's most charming exhibition halls.

A significant part of the workmanship in the structure (a previous theater) is portable and coin-worked, so have a couple of euro coins in your pockets when you go. You know how you can never get a taxi when it's pouring? Pop a coin into Dalí's own 1941 Cadillac, and it rains inside the vehicle.

Another feature is the Mae West room. From simply the correct spot, you'll see that the couch lips, chimney nostrils, painting eyes, and drapery hair meet up to make the substance of the sultry entertainer. Meandering around this spot, I can't resist pondering: am I insane, or is it Dalí? The craftsman himself is buried in a grave underneath middle of everyone's attention.

Close by Cadaqués is an ocean side diamond at the Spain's easternmost tip. With whitewashed structures, a delicate sea breeze, and marvelous straight perspectives, Cadaqués is untainted and remote. It has no train administration and just a modest entry street that impasse. (Transports and cabs interface it to Figueres, however in the event that meeting Barcelona with no vehicle, I would love to go Sitges.)

Most explorers in Cadaqués are here for the purposes of the home that Dalí imparted to his better half (and dream) Function. Together they changed over an angler's home — around a 20-minute stroll from the downtown area — into their half permanent living arrangement, separating their time between New York, Paris, and Cadaqués. It was at this place where Dalí did his best work, and I think of it as the most intriguing home of a perished character in the entire Europe. (It's extremely famous and just permits eight guests one after another for accompanied visits, so you should get reservations online ahead of time.) However Dalí was brought up in Figueres, as a child, he enjoys his summers here in the family lodge, where he was captivated by the rough scene, which would later turn out to be the background for some, Surrealist canvases.

Cadaqués generally offers little in the method for sights, however the old town is amazingly trademarked. I like to walk around the water from the Dalí statue on the sea shore, past the gambling club where time stops, and appreciate the "elephant trees" imported from Cuba (numerous Catalans briefly migrated to Cuba during the time it was under Spanish guideline in the nineteenth century). Tough, the Jewish Quarter is as yet rich with remnants of the solid Jewish people group that flourished in Spain until 1492. That is when Christian obsession (gone wild with the last triumph over the Fields) prompted the ejection of Muslims and Jews from Catholic Spain. At the highest point of town, the Congregation of Santa Clause Maria provides ordering perspectives on Cadaqués. Inside, a rich Elaborate special raised area highlights 365 cut figures canvassed in gold, which was mined from America.

On the off chance that you essentially need to kick back without a motivation, go to inviting Sitges, which has visit 30-minute train administration from Barcelona. With a much more slow heartbeat than Barcelona, this retreat town southwest of the city is an ideal break from touring. Sitges has fly set status, however it's clung to its Old World appeal while figuring out how to be both family-and gay accommodating.

There are Modernista-style manors here and a couple of commendable little exhibition halls, however I suggest simply jabbing around the old town's whitewashed lanes, packed with bistros and boutiques. At that point head for the water to absorb the sun, ocean, and sand.

Nine sea shores, isolated by jetties, expand southward from town (the last three are close and bay like). Walk around the shoreline promenade or lease a sea shore seat for some outrageous unwinding. En route, you'll get a rich selection of eateries and beachfront bars or chiringuitos for the paella, tapas as well as beverages.

In the event that you opt to pay a visit during one of Sitges' two major celebrations, you might be able to see groups of castellers contending to develop human pyramids to go for about sixty feet high. The celebrations are St. Tecla in late September, and St. Bartholomew in late August.

Adjusting on the shoulders of the individuals underneath, the castellers are made a decision by how rapidly they can collect and bring down their kin towers. Nobody is extremely certain how this peculiar convention got its beginning, however it's an ideal impression of the locale's group building twisted.

Jumping out of Barcelona for the day is simple. Regardless of whether you encounter the hallowed, the dreamlike, or the ocean side, you'll come back to the city energized and prepared for anything it has available.

Chapter 4: What Else to Notice?

Life in Barcelona is an unmistakable blend of Madrid-style love of life and Parisian class and taste. Spain's second-greatest city is one of the most sizzling vacationer goals in Europe nowadays, with more than 7.5 million guests every year, so its famous person on foot lanes can end up human automobile overloads.

Disregarding what can be awful groups, there's bounty to appreciate. Wherever you go, you'll see the city's design as bright, energetic, and exceptional. Lines of balanced ironwork galleries are punctuated with whimsical subtleties: cove windows, turrets, painted tiles, hanging lamps, bloom boxes, and cut reliefs.

At different focuses in its history, this glad city has been a Roman retirement settlement, an oceanic power, a dynamo of the Mechanical Age, and a urban ideal example for innovation. Today it cobbles together every one of these components into an exceptional culture.

Barcelona is the capital of Spain's Catalunya district. Local people pride themselves on their diverse language and talk continually and intensely about autonomy. Furthermore, with each visit, I hear increasingly Catalan and less Spanish. Conversing with my companions in Barcelona about the common sense of having their kids learn Catalan — leaving them with a local tongue that under 10 million individuals talk in a forceful and worldwide world — none of them doubted the thought. Obviously they speak Catalan... they are Catalans. What's more, they communicate in Spanish and English too — they're accomplished Europeans.

The notorious principle square, Plaça de Catalunya, sits at Barcelona's inside, separating the more established and fresher pieces of town. Beneath the square is the Old City, with the road called the Ramblas running down to the harbor. This Catalan Champs-Elysées has for some time been a quintessential Barcelona experience. Be that as it may, with present day wealth and the ascent of the travel industry, the appeal of the Ramblas is everything except dead. The elderly people men perusing their papers, the winged creature and blossom markets, and the nearby shops are presently supplanted by shabby low-end vacationer shops.

Barcelona's most notable neighborhood is the Barri Gòtic, with a fourteenth century church building as its navel. Today, the territory is a tangled-yet-welcoming get sack of terrific squares, schoolyards, Craftsmanship Nouveau customer facing facades, smelly garbage shops, tasteful classical shops, and road performers strumming Catalan people tunes. While the ongoing lifting of lease control has caused a large number of the bygone era shops to crease, fortunately the character of this quarter endures.

For an edgier cut of the city, step just past the Barri Gòtic into the area called El Conceived (a.k.a. "La Ribera"). This bohemian-chic area highlights out of control shops, upscale bistros and wine bars serving slyly made tapas, a beautiful market lobby, one of a kind boutiques, and one of Barcelona's top exhibition halls, the Museu Picasso.

Over the Old City, past the clamoring Plaça de Catalunya center, is the rich Eixample area. A lot of Barcelona's Modernista design is found here — particularly three beautiful exteriors worked toward the finish of the nineteenth century that seek consideration: Casa Batlló, Casa Amatller, and Casa Lleó. Since the manors look as if they are attempting to exceed each other in inventive turns, local people have named them the "Square of Strife."

The Eixample is additionally home to popular Catalan modeler Antoni Gaudí's La Pedrera (a.k.a. Casa Milà), with its much-shot crazy ride of liquefying dessert overhang. This is Barcelona's quintessential Modernista building and Gaudí's last significant work before he devoted his last a long time to the Sagrada Família.

Sagrada Família (Sacred Family Church) is Gaudí's incomplete artful culmination. It flaunts intense, natural design and stylistic theme all around — from its softening Greatness Veneer to its skull-like Enthusiasm Exterior to its rainforest-esque inside. Gaudí toiled on the Sagrada Família for a long time, from 1883 until his demise in 1926. From that point forward, development has pushed ahead in fits and starts. In 2010, the principle nave was done enough to have a sanctification Mass by the pope. As I ventured inside on my last visit, the brightness of Gaudí's vision made for elevated love in the about finished nave.

The present primary difficulties for this epic work-in-progress: develop the tallest church tower at any point fabricated, guarantee that development can withstand the vibrations from expedient trains thundering underneath, and figure out how to purchase out apartment suite proprietors to satisfy Gaudí's vision of an amazing esplanade moving toward the congregation. The objective to complete the congregation by the 100th commemoration of Gaudí's demise, in 2026, may appear to be excessively hopeful. Be that as it may, with cash from a large number of guests pouring in every year (the confirmation is expensive — yet you know it's for an energizing reason), it shows up progressively realistic as time passes by. I've long stated, "If there's one structure I'd at present prefer to find in Europe, it's Gaudí's Sagrada Família church in Barcelona... wrapped up."

With frame of mind in its craft, culture, and legislative issues, Barcelona — notwithstanding its traveler swarms — is where you're probably going to wave the nearby banner and proclaim, alongside its occupants, "Visca Catalunya!"

Barcelona remains the subsequent city in Spain, and headquarters of the pleased and particular district of Catalunya. Now that the much dreaded autocracy of Franco forgotten, the inventive and autonomous soul of Catalan is having some fantastic luck. It is one of the most energetic corners in this side of the larger European continent. Hosts several people too.

In Barcelona a neighborhood let me know "Catalan is Spain's Quebec." Going here you perceive how the individuals of Catalan have a partiality for other "stateless countries." Local people do not really care to consider their side of Spanish Iberia a "district".

These people insist that they are a "country without a state." They also have a proclivity for other individuals who were unable to attain their freedom when the national limits were drawn. They co-existed with several countries — discovering Galacian and Basque bars somewhat more engaging when compared to the ordinary Spanish bars.

Roman state, a latter-day Visigothic capital, and a fourteenth century sea influence. Also, past its extraordinary sights, make certain to welcome the city's rich feeling of style and the skill just seen in the Mediterranean.

The fundamental square of the city, Plaça de Catalunya, is the focal point of therefore the people residing in Catalunya. It's an exuberant people scene for anybody. The whole square is embellished with carved images that are respecting significant Catalans. There is a special language that is spoken in Catalunya — which local people fly gladly... and in solitude from the condos.

Catalunya has frequently been inconsistent with the government leaders based in Madrid. Harking back to the 1930s this territory became the final bunches of obstruction against the Fundamentalist despot Francisco Franco. At the point Franco at last regained power, he rebuffed the district with 4 many years of restraint. Within that duration, local people were restricted against moving their banner. To demonstrate their soul, the Barcelona soccer group banner was flown.

Indeed, even Barcelona's ATM machines were in harmony with the European group of "Stateless Countries." They offer the right selection of dialects: Alongside Points, Castellano, and Frances you'll generally discover other hidden treasures in the region. Despite the fact that there's imaginable not one ATM client a year who might talk just Gallec or Euskera, they offered them the semantic regard that they would seek after in an outside land.

Barcelona residents assemble before their house of God to commend their locale by moving the conventional sardana every Sunday. Conventional instruments — which bring out the battle these individuals have pursued during that time to keep their way of life.

The language of the Catalan is irreversibly attached to the background and soul of the Catalan individuals. From the finish of the Franco's regime, delighted in a gigantic rebirth. It is the main language of the neighborhood institutions and nowadays the first language of the kids here is Catalan, and the second one is Spanish.

An ongoing prosperity has raised the whole place. A trace of threat in the Barri Gòtic neighborhood can no longer been seen. I recall the city's fundamental lane, the Ramblas. As of now, they are the wandering groups of hooligans who operate the high-vitality, amazingly jittery shell games. Very anxious men hurry their dodgy peas with spotters tough and downhill, and a full group of peddlers. It's astonishing there are sufficient tricks in the city.

Whereas keepsake shops and hordes of vacationers have weakened the Ramblas' previous tastefulness, regardless it provides an engaging spot to witness the jubilee of life in

Barcelona. Be that as it may, focus. Any place individuals bar to gape, petty thieves are grinding away. I believe you are as prone to be pickpocketed in the city— particularly on the Ramblas — and about anyplace in the Europe. On the off chance that you take a break for any disturbance or exhibition.

My feature with this Barcelona visit was less energizing — pimientos de Padrón, delicately served steaming. They're a sort of Russian roulette designed for the ones who would enjoy, as the anxious eater realizes that now and again you hit an overly hot pepper.

Scarcely any urban areas so effectively charm guests with the magnificence and Barcelona kind of flavor. Life rises in its tight, back streets, terrific lanes, and exquisite current locale. Whereas Barcelona boasts of a celebrated past — from the province of Rome to fourteenth century sea control — it's charming to toss out the archives and simply float all over the city.

There is an excellent avenue that will take you from rich to unpleasant in a one-mile, thirty-minute walk.

The Ramblas always signifies "stream" in Arabic, is a perpetual current of individuals and activity. You'll pontoon the stream of life in Barcelona on the other side of a fantastic show house, lavish bistros, resigned whores, specialists, road emulates, an outside flying creature market, as well as the pickpockets. At the energetic produce advertise, local people buy stuff in the first part of the day generally advantageous and the best meat, organic product, as well as vegetables. They state on the off chance that you can't discover it in the Boqueria.

Ramblas's east side is the Gothic quarter, as well as Barcelona's Barri Gòtic that revolves around the goliath church. The thin boulevards that encompass the church building are a clamoring universe of kiosks, bars, and not forgetting nightlife pressed into tight, paths and unfamiliar yards. Simply above road level is just a fashioned iron overhangs whose bars scarcely contain their local wildernesses.

An imaginative soul is a piece of the back and forth movement of day-by-day life in Barcelona. His plans are discovered everywhere throughout the city, from wall paintings to mobiles to the logo of La Caixa bank.

The Picasso Historical center is by a wide margin the best gathering of the craftsman's operations in Spain. Watching young, reasonable craftsmanship, you will be more readily value the virtuoso of his later, progressively dynamic workmanship.

For a reviving short pause from the thick old town, move north next to cutting edge Eixample area has broad walkways, chic shops, smooth shade trees, and Craftsmanship Nouveau ruffles. Barcelona was breaking from its medieval dividers by the 1850s, thus another town — called the Eixample ("development") — was spread out in a network design. The first vision was a populist one: Every twenty square locale was to have its very own medical clinic and enormous park, schools, markets and childcare focuses.

However, after some time the Eixample turned into a grandstand for affluent occupants and the planners, who transformed the prospering Craftsmanship, their personal image of ornamental structure. Structures blossom with trademark brilliant, verdant, and streaming shapes in entryways, passageways, exteriors, and roofs.

Barcelona's most well known Modernista craftsman, Antoni Gaudí, made compositional dreams that are a peculiar blanket of running peaks and natural bends. A quintessential case of Casa Milà has dividers of a whimsical and wavy stone, undulating housetop, where a total of thirty fireplaces enjoy the game of volleyball with the mists. A green-blue artistic dotted veneer at Casa Batlio, tibia-esque columns, and shell-like galleries are motivated naturally, whereas the humpback roofline proposes a peaking mythical beast's back.

Be that as it may, Gaudí's most constant work is the endlessly incomplete Sagrada Família, with its fiercely imaginative, indisputably natural curves and towers. The Nativity Veneer, the main piece of the congregation basically finished in his lifetime, demonstrates the engineer's unique vision. Blending the natural pizazz of Modernisme, a noteworthy case of his indisputable style is created.

Nearby specialists frequently wrap up their professions by placing in several years taking a shot at the venture. The congregation should be finished in the next six years, which denotes the hundredth commemoration of the demise of Gaudí. It could occur — following 3 many years of visits, I have had an opportunity to see significant improvement. Your confirmation helps pay for the progressing development.

Gaudí fans likewise appreciate the craftsman's enchantment in the vivid; a thirty-section of land peak garden after it was proposed to be a sixty-habitation lodging venture, a sort of enclosed network. Covered with whimsical mosaics and dabbed with figures (counting a goliath tiled reptile), this park is an incredible spot to top the day.

From workmanship to nourishment to business sectors, Barcelona has some expertise in enthusiastic — and that is the reason it's such a hit with voyagers.

I'm remaining on a modest gallery disregarding the Occasions Square of the entire

Spain — Madrid's Puerta del Sol. Inside a ten-minute walk I can visit probably the best royal residence in Europe — Madrid's Illustrious Castle, a definitive town square — Court Civic chairman, or my preferred accumulation of depictions within any rooftop in such places like the Prado Historical center.

Much the same as in New York's Occasions Square jams in Madrid this square on New Year's Eve while the remainder of Spain watches the activity on television. As Spain's "Enormous Ben" on the senator's office tolls multiple times, Madrileños eat a single grape for each ring to bring good karma via every one of the following a year.

In any case, not at all like New York's well-known social affair space, this square — like such a significant number of in Europe — has now migrated to a more park-setup individuals zone. It is what makes Madrid decent. Vehicle traffic has been constrained (made conceivable by the superb open transportation framework), giving the fine old structures a chance to flaunt their unique style in an enticing, wide-open setting.

All there Puerta del Sol, I will do a rush voyage through three noteworthy sights. I begin by walking around the Regal Castle that I think about Europe's third most noteworthy royal residence (after Versailles, close to Paris, and Schönbrunn in

Vienna). Throughout the years, I have likely visited it in any event multiple times — and I generally adapt all the more entrancing realities to incorporate into my manual.

It's huge — in excess of 2,000 rooms, with huge amounts of extravagant woven artworks, a lord's payoff of ceiling fixtures, extremely valuable porcelain, and bronze stylistic theme canvassed in gold leaf. Whereas nowadays the imperial family lives in a house a couple of miles away, this spot still capacities as a regal castle, and is utilized for formal state gatherings, regal weddings, and travelers' fantasies.

One feature is the position of authority room, where red velvet dividers, frescoes and lions of Spanish scenes shows the government in an extravagant mob. Another eye-plug is the eating corridor, where the ruler can engage upwards of 144 visitors at a bowling path size table. The roof fresco portrays Christopher Columbus stooping before Isabel and Ferdinand, exhibiting intriguing keepsakes and his New World "companions" to the regal couple.

Square Civic chairman is next stop — a stately, without traffic lump of seventeenth century Spain. Each side of the square is a special uniform, as though an amazing royal residence were turned back to front. In the case of spending time with old companions, getting a charge out of some espresso, or finding a fortune at the morning coin show, it's an engaging spot where individuals accumulate.

Bronze reliefs under the lampposts show how upon this stage, quite a bit of Spanish history was played out. The square once facilitated bullfights. It was the area of ages of pre-Loaned jamboree joy. Furthermore, during the Examination, many speculated blasphemers were attempted here and rebuffed by being choked or consumed at the stake. Fortunately, the mercilessness of the Investigation is a distant memory.

My last stop is the Prado Historical center, which holds my preferred gathering of depictions anyplace. These works of art give an eye-satisfying outline of Spain's rich history, from its Brilliant Age through its moderate blur.

The Prado is the spot to appreciate the incomparable Spanish painter Francisco de Goya. You can finish this mind-boggling man an amazing phases — from loyal court painter, to political dissident and outrage producer, to the baffled virtuoso of his "dark works of art." It's likewise the home of Diego Velázquez's Las Meninas, regarded by some to be the world's best painting, time frame. Notwithstanding Spanish works, you'll discover sketches by Flemish and Italian bosses, including Hieronymus Bosch's fantastical Nursery of Natural Joys altarpiece.

Within excess of three thousand canvases, including whole rooms of artful culminations by genius painters, the Prado is able to be overpowering. A $215 million development, finished in 2007, made this exhibition hall more guests inviting. Another wing holds a cutting edge bistro, theater, and blessing shop — opening up display space in the first working for more workmanship. In any case, regardless it becomes busy. To maintain a strategic distance from the swarms, remember that noon and weekdays are commonly less pressed. It's constantly packed on nights, when it's free following 6 p.m., and on ends of the week; it merits paying the section cost on different days to have your entire space.

As I stroll back to my inn on the Puerta del Sol, I think about this clamoring capital — Europe's most elevated, at two thousand feet. In spite of the monetary vulnerability, the present Madrid is dynamic. Indeed, even the living-statue road entertainers have a twinkle in their eyes. Energetic Madrid has enough road singing, partying like a rock star, and people-watching imperativeness to offer any guest a lift. After each outing to this energizing city, the impression I bring home is that of a flourishing people with a suffering society.

I prefer taking in European history by walking an area, the same manner a person would do while at the beach.

Grabbing pieces of a spot's far off past, it is actually conceivable to sort out startling conversations. The most admired Jewish quarters are perfect spots for the feat.

The Jewish history in the Europe is overwhelmed by Holocaust and the severe abuse and killing of Jews. It is the Nazis who did that. Those aggravating occasions — deplorably and horrendously — at times cloud the a lot more established history of the Jews in Europe. Be that as it may, different places compensate guests with intriguing looks into the extravagance and life span of the culture of the Jews.

One known Jewish quarter is Cordoba, the murmurs with history. Found in the touristy downtown area and the piece of town, the side paths draw their memory from the great Medieval times. Back then, Jews succeeded under the great resistance of the decision Islamic caliphate.

The unique design is safeguarded by the quarter, with limited boulevards cleared with waterway stone cobbles and fixed with whitewashed, and thick dividers. At the core lies a little, antiquated synagogue, worked in the mid-1300s. It is a remarkably otherworldly spot, inconspicuously finished with cut twining blossoms. Jews asked here up to their last ejection in 1492 from Spain. Working as a congregation, an emergency clinic, and an organization corridor, the structure's unique capacity was discovered distinctly again in the late nineteenth century.

Only a couple of steps away, in a reestablished fourteenth century home, where the Casa de Sefarad. The historical center features the past of Córdoba's as a scholarly focus, as well as the life of the incomparable Jewish savant, Moses Maimonides. Guide for the bewildered, Maimonides' best-known works, has motivated armies of clearness looking for vacationers to rub the statue foot down the road.

Prague's Josefov neighborhood is one of the most dominant spots for encountering Jewish history. Jews arrived at Prague as quite a while in the past as the tenth century, filling in as shippers and merchants. As they thrived here, they manufactured homes and synagogues. In any case, they were likewise oppressed throughout the hundreds of years — enduring segregation, dangerous massacres, and Nazi severity.

Currently, Prague hosts small amount of the Jewish populace present before 1940. However minimal Josefov has a portion of Europe's most significant Jewish locations, with some few synagogues from the sixteenth and seventeenth hundreds of years. Together, they work as recorded and social historical centers whose displays give an intensive lesson in the traditions and conventions of the Jews.

A single synagogue is currently working as a moving dedication. When the private spot of love for a noticeable sixteenth century family, the pale dividers are secured with close to 100,000 titles, written by hand to respect and recollect Czech Jews killed in the 2nd world war.

Josefov is simply behind the Pinkas. For more than 300 years, it was the main graveyard took into consideration the Prague's Jews. In the absence of sufficient space, they layered the graves up to ten profound, making the ground to rise up above the road level. It's a mysteriously pleasant spot, with regarded headstones tidied with heaps of rocks, an indication of regard.

In current occasions, most of Europe's Jews resided in Poland, and their political and social bases were Kraków's Kazimierz areas. Albeit couple of Jews stay there, the soul of their conventions continues on in a bunch of synagogues, graveyards, and eateries.

Its caged avenues and special structures have persevered more through generous disregard than astute arranging. Be that as it may, that is made the lease modest, drawing in a diletantish group and youthful business people. Crowds of youthful revelers obstruct the boulevards after dim, the beats blending in with some great music.

One of the numerous spots where the huge occasions of Second World War met with the lives of common individuals is Kazimiers. The representative Oskar Schindler managed his lacquer processing plant close here all through the war — and spared the lives of in excess of so many of his Jewish specialists. Presently, perhaps the best exhibition hall concerning the Nazi occupation fills the structure with Schindler and his representatives operated.

The universe of Jews in the Europe can likewise be found in its nourishment.

Crosswise over Europe, the legacy of age-old quarters of the Jews allures astute explorers. Pay them a visit to discover living connects to a rich.

Every July, a several clubbers throng into Pamplona, Spain, for the rowdy San Fermín celebrations. They result in these present circumstances pleased town in the Pyrenees lower regions for music, firecrackers, and fun. Yet, a large portion of all pushes themselves into the six angry bulls way.

Initially celebrated as a holy person's blowout day, the celebration currently keeps running for nine days, from July the 6th to the 14th. Every morning at eight o'clock, the bulls are released on the city roads with Spaniards over that country following each bend and turn on live TV.

Mozos, similar to Spanish bullfighting fans, regard the bull. The creature speaks to control, life, the extraordinary wild. Ernest Hemingway, who originally went to the celebration in 1923, comprehended. He composed that he delighted in watching two wild creatures run together — one on two legs, the other on four.

In spite of the fact that they are able to put on anything, and the mozos customarily put on white jeans, with red handkerchiefs tied in their necks and midriffs. 2 seniors clarify the white and red uniform: One of them allude that it is to respect San Fermín, a holy person who was martyred; different says that the sprinters put on clothes like the butchers who started this custom. (

An influx of vitality floods through the roads every morning as the beginning time draws near. My film team and myself were at an ongoing celebration, positioned at a focal point along a strong boundary where it'd be easy for the bulls to go obscuring by. (The occasion spreads out so rapidly that we recorded it on two mornings to get enough film.) Each morning, observers start amassing at the break of day. For huge numbers of the merrymakers, early morning is only the last part of a night of celebrating.

As spectators pack the side rear entryways, the mozos racer for an ideal situation in the city. For genuine sprinters, this resembles surfing: You would like to get a decent wave and ride it. A decent run keeps going just 15 or 20 seconds. You realize you are truly running with the bull when you feel the breath of the creature on your jeans.

Taking after several pogo sticks, an ocean of sprinters immediately starts bouncing all.

Just in the same manner an oddity wave walloping seashore, the bulls hurry over. By the time the bulls pursue the road, the mozos try to spread remain out before the roaring crowd, plunging off the beaten path at last.

A bull turns out to be most hazardous when isolated from the group. Thus, a couple of cow — who are more settled and slower — are discharged. There is no more prominent shame in this culture as opposed to might suspect you've kept running with a bull, just to acknowledge later that you really kept running with a cow.

At that point, all of a sudden, the bulls are no more. Individuals lift up, and it is finished. Blocked shops open up, and the timber wall are brought down and stacked. Similar to the custom, members drop into a bar following the running, eat, and together watch the rerun of the whole display on television — each of its 131 seconds.

Every year, many individuals are gutted, stomped on, or generally harmed during the occasion. A mozos who falls ought to never show signs of improvement to be stomped on by six bulls than to be gutted by one. While bulls in the course of the only remaining century have murdered 15 sprinters, unquestionably more celebration goers have been impeded from too much use of liquor. The celebration means gathering Pamplona.

It's amusing to track with in the real foot-and footsteps of the members. The course is always set apart by signals. The most hair-raising focuses is at the move toward the road named La Estafeta, start heading downhill, frequently losing their parity and sliding into the blockades. At the point when the bulls aren't running, La Estafeta is one of the most engaging lanes in Pamplona, home to the absolute best tapas bars around the local area.

At the point when the romping celebration finishes up at 12 PM on July 14, Pomplona's townspeople assemble before City Corridor, light candles, and sing their pitiful melody, "Pobre de Mí:" "Poor me, the Party de San Fermín has finished."

Roosted on a high edge, the inconceivably curious hobbit village of O Cebreiro invites guests to Galicia — an uneven, moist, green locale in northwest Spain that feels dubiously Irish. O Cebreiro is a time-travel to an uncomplicated, practically ancient past, when individuals lived exceptionally near nature, in stone igloos with covered rooftops. With clearing sees over the verdant however cruel Galician scene, O Cebreiro (articulated gracious theh-Whinny roh) is always pounded by the absolute fiercest climate in Spain.

O Cebreiro scents like wood flames, excrement, and explorer B.O. The town is shared by two gatherings: a couple of basic townspeople, who rooster their heads curiously when gotten some information about brand new developments like email, and fatigued Camino de Santiago pioneers on an adrenaline high after at last arriving at Galicia. O Cebreiro marks the last stretch of their month-long, 450-mile journey to the city of Santiago de Compostela, along the Camino de Santiago (or Method for St. James). The town's canines bark at one another regionally from over the road, totally overlooking the explorers who routinely walk through town.

To get a kind of the nearby culture, get a bite or drink at one of the about six humble bar/eateries, which feed explorers and different guests generous Galician cooking in a smoky environment. One nearby strength is caldo galego, a customary soup that initially originated from the extra stock used to set up an intricate Sunday feast (cabbage or grelos, potatoes, etc). It's not very energizing, however it provides comfort on a stormy day.

In the event that you hear something that seems like, however isn't exactly Spanish, it's Galego — the unmistakable language of Galicia. A blend among Portuguese and Spanish, Galego has step by step developed to sound increasingly like the last mentioned. The most obvious contrast is the adjustment in articles: el and la become o and a — so the huge Galician city La Coruña is known as "A Coruña" around here. The Spanish welcome buenos días is bos días in Galego. In the event that you need to intrigue a neighborhood, state graciñas (grah-THEEN-yahs) — a super-gracious bless your heart.

To perceive how nearby locals used to live, visit the pallozas. From Celtic occasions 1,500 years back, until the 1960s, the townspeople of O Cebreiro shacked in these modest, round stone cottages with topped covered rooftops. Three of the nine enduring pallozas have been transformed into an approximately run gallery, where guests can find out about the ways of life of the individuals who lived in the hovels.

After entering a palloza, which ordinarily housed twelve individuals (and their creatures), you'll discover two basic rooms: the main "private" room in the house, having a place with the guardians, and a living region around a modest flame. Encompassing the flame are smart seats (which were additionally utilized as hard beds) with draw down counters so they could serve as a table at supper time. Cooking was done over the flame utilizing a chain swinging from a major shaft, while monster dark metal spirals suspended from the roof were utilized to smoke chorizo.

Connected to the living zone is a scaled down "stable," where creatures lived on the lower level, and individuals — kept warm by all that domesticated animals body heat — dozed on the upper level. Because of the perfect protection given by the cover, and the glow from the flame and creatures, it was toasty even through the troublesome winter.

In O Cebreiro, all streets lead to the town church. Established in the year 836, Santa Clause María la Genuine (Illustrious St. Mary's) is as far as anyone knows the most seasoned church on the whole French Street of the Camino de Santiago. The inside of this pre-Romanesque structure is shockingly roomy, however extremely straightforward. The structure is really inserted into the ground, with indented floors that additional assurance against winter storms. At a work area, a representative stamps travelers' accreditations and sells votive candles.

As managed by antiquated custom, the baptistery is isolated from the primary piece of the congregation, with its mammoth and exceptionally harsh textual style utilized for drenching submersions. In the sanctuary to one side of the fundamental raised area is a much-loved twelfth century brilliant vessel and reliquary, which holds things identifying with a neighborhood supernatural occurrence: A worker from a close by town overcame a wild winter blizzard to result in these present circumstances church for the Eucharist. The minister laughed at his commitment, just to find that the host and wine had physically transformed into the body and blood of Christ, recoloring the materials underneath them — which are presently in the silver box.

To get way off the beaten track, appreciate Spain getting it done by "playing traveler" for a couple of hours here in hauntingly lovely O Cebreiro.

Remaining on the primary Santiago de Compostela Square. With burned from the sun faces and frayed strolling sticks, they finish up their long trek by stepping on a scallop shell cut into the asphalt before the city's heavenly church building. For over 100 years, this house of God in Spain's northwest corner of Spain has been the ceremonial last advance for pioneers who've climbed here from holy places in Paris and all over Europe. Today, most go for a month to stroll the 450 miles from the French border town of Holy person Jean-Pied-de-Port.

To appreciate the scene, be on the square around 10 a.m. The keep going medium-term stop on the Camino (or journey) is two miles away, and most pioneers land at the church building in time for the 12:00 Mass. It's extraordinary enjoyable to visit with pioneers who've quite recently finished their voyage. They appear to be extremely focused, and checked out the significant things in life...like setting aside some effort to converse with others.

James, Santiago's namesake and image, was a Christian evangelist — one of Jesus' unique "fishers of men." Yet making a decision from the manner in which he's depicted here, his fundamental movement was decapitating Muslims with his bustling sword. Propagandistic statues of James are all over town — riding in from paradise to enable the Spaniards to vanquish the Muslim Fields.

Police protect the square. Security here has been tight as far back as September 11, 2001 — and considerably more so since Walk 11, 2004, when Madrid's passenger trains were shelled. Santiago's house of prayer, as one of the main journey locales in The Christian world, is a prominent objective for Islamic fundamentalists. It doesn't support that St. James is portrayed rejoicing in light of butchering Muslims.

Students of history figure the "disclosure" of the remaining parts of St. James in Spain was a medieval deception. It was intended to revitalize Europe against the Muslim Fields, who had attacked Spain and were taking steps to proceed into Europe. With St. James — a.k.a. "the Field Slayer" — covered in Iberia, all of Europe would ascend to drive the Muslims over into Africa...which, following a centuries-in length "Reconquista," they at long last did in 1492.

This uproar goes back around 1,200 years to a priest who pursued a field of stars (presumably the Smooth Way) to this far off corner of Europe and found what gave off an impression of being the missing tomb of St. James. Church pioneers announced that St. James' relics had been discovered, fabricated a congregation, and named the spot Santiago (St. James) de Compostela (campo de estrellas, or "field of stars").

Envision you're a medieval traveler. You've quite recently strolled from Paris — in excess of 700 miles — to arrive at this church building. Your objective: to demand the assistance of St. James in recuperating from a disease. Or on the other hand possibly you've come to respect the desire of a perishing relative...or to be excused for your wrongdoings. Whatever the explanation, you realize the pope guaranteed that any individual who strolled to Santiago in a Heavenly Year, admitted their wrongdoings, and took communion here would be excused.

Following quite a while of climbing, the tower of the church comes into view and celebration enlivens your worn out pace. At long last you remain upon the shell in the asphalt and look up at the remarkable house of God. You step inside, squint down the nave, and see the statue of St. James that denotes his tomb.

Bowing at the silver tomb of St. James, you ask and make your solicitation. At that point you climb the stairs behind the special stepped area up to the holy person's quite loved statue — plated and built up with valuable jewels — and hang tight to grasp him from behind while looking fortunately out over the basilica. You have finished the Camino de Santiago.

Strolling the Method for St. James has changed minimal throughout the hundreds of years. The rigging still incorporates a shroud, a floppy cap, a mobile stick, a gourd (for drinking from wells), and a scallop shell (symbolizing where you're going).

The walk itself is a sort of cottage jumping. At customary interims along the course, you'll experience humble government-financed inns called albergues, where pioneers can rest for the evening (free bunks, however little gift frequently mentioned).

As of late the course has delighted in a colossal renaissance of enthusiasm, with almost 100,000 explorers trekking to Santiago a year ago. Bikers and steed riders are currently joining explorers.

Regardless of whether you climb the whole course or simply the last stretch — or regardless of whether you're only there to vicariously appreciate the rush of the most recent in a thousand years of travelers completing the Camino de Santiago — it's an encounter that will remain with you for eternity.

My guide Roberto met me at Madrid's air terminal, we leased a vehicle, and minutes after the fact, we were southbound on the road, drenched in the immensity of La Mancha. It's an extreme territory. A windmill — endured into an unpleasant minimal futile stub — still topped its stormy slope.

We flew into a rural truck stop for lunch. As I inclined toward my ham sandwich, my voyaging soul did a little jump and I thought, truly, España! My international ID had been stepped, however I hadn't generally landed until that minute, when my teeth got through the fresh hull of my cushy crisp roll... and hit jamón.

That prosciutto-like ham, dry-restored and matured from upbeat, oak seed bolstered pigs, has a striking flavor that exemplifies the natural force of the Spanish culture. Restored ham hawks — conditioned legs with pointed toes — are found in each bar. Like epicureans of fine wine, Spaniards banter the benefits of various types of pigs, their weight control plans, and the nature of the restoring. In Spain, jamón is in excess of a nourishment; it's a lifestyle. Spaniards treasure recollections of Grandpa during Christmas, meagerly cutting a ham upheld in a jamonero (ham-pawn holder), similarly as we prize the turkey cutting at Thanksgiving. To test this delicacy without the significant expense label you'll discover in cafés, go to a nearby market and request 100 grams of top-quality ham; appreciate it as a cookout with red wine and a roll.

Beside such ham, 700 years of Muslim standard left its blemish on the Spanish food. The Fields were extraordinary horticulturists and acquainted Spain with new herbs and flavors — a heritage that is all around spoken to in paella. Customary Center Eastern saffron consolidates with rice, fish, wiener, and chicken for a formula that is quintessentially Spanish.

Each area of Spain has fortes worth enjoying. La Mancha is known for its jamón as well as for pisto, a ratatouille-like dish usually presented with quail eggs. In Catalunya, there's fideuà, a dainty, season injected noodle presented with fish, and arròs negre, dark rice cooked in squid ink. Along the North Atlantic, Asturias joins fish with generous mountain grub, including mammoth white faba beans and the ground-breaking Roquefort-like cabrales cheddar. Green, stormy Galicia in the northwest is known for octopus, slashed up and served tidied with paprika. The district's broiled green pimientos de Padrón are delectable and precarious, offering a sort of Russian roulette — around one of every ten of these little peppers is fiery hot.

Seemingly the culinary capital of Spain is San Sebastián, in Basque Nation, with welcoming tapas bars (they're called pintxos here) that show a dazzling cluster of assistance yourself treats. Top dishes incorporate creepy crawly crab, delicious anchovies, and fish stew. Simply snatch what you like from the platters at the bar; when it's a great opportunity to settle up, the server will tally the toothpicks on your plate.

In Spain, feast segments are unique in relation to what we're utilized to. It's surprising to discover an eatery that recognizes "starters" and "fundamental dishes." Rather, most cafés serve their dishes in full segments called raciones, or in littler half-servings, media-raciones. Requesting media-raciones is a simple path for you and your movement accomplice to expand your tasting background (two individuals can top off on four media-raciones). Try not to wash it down with a glass of fundamental red wine (tinto); rather, request un crianza — for just some extra, you'll get a quality, matured wine.

Numerous guests locate the Spanish eating calendar disappointing. Lunch, the biggest feast of the day, is eaten around 3 p.m. Numerous Spaniards have a bocadillo (roll sandwich) around 11 a.m. to cross over any barrier between their espresso and-move breakfast and late lunch. Since most Spanish go to work until half past seven, a light dinner at nine or ten p.m. is average. By and large no self-regarding casa de comidas ("place of eating" — when you see this, you can wager it's a decent, customary restaurant) serves snacks and suppers at American hours.

To eat well whenever, and inside even the most secure spending plan, duck into a tapas bar and manufacture a light feast out of hors d'oeuvres. While I by and large go for the provincial old bars, Roberto acquainted me with a spot that puts a contemporary turn on conventional tapas. We pretty much ate our way through the whole rundown of day by day specials: asparagus snowed in with Manchego cheddar, fragile cod-cheek sandwiches, and zesty pulled pork.

What's more, three days into my Spain trip, it was clear I was settling in perfectly. I battled to the highest point of a slope topping château ruin in Castille. Regaining some composure, I overviewed the tremendous territory and it appeared my perspiration accompanied a swoon whiff of jamón.

Madrid is the center of Spain. This cutting edge capital — Europe's most elevated, at in excess of 2,000 feet — has a populace of 3.2 million. Like its kin, the city is generally youthful. 100 years prior, Madrid had just 400,000 inhabitants — so most of the present Madrid is current spread encompassing an unblemished, simple to-explore memorable center.

When known basically for its historical centers, royal residences, and tapas bars, the cityscape of Madrid is evolving. To help its offers to have the 2012 and 2016 Olympics, the city started some enormous ventures of urban-improvement. Despite the fact that it lost the two offers (to London and after that Rio de Janeiro), the development proceeds as though the city had won — inhabitants love to check out all the new squares, walker boulevards, expressway passages, parks, and Metro stations springing up. Indeed, even in the wake of being ignored for soccer's 2018 World Cup, hopeful people are peering toward coming Olympics offers, giving the city a reason to keep up the development.

Madrid's driven plans achieved the formation of a magnificent person on foot traversing the city from the Prado Exhibition hall to the Regal Castle. Walking around Calle de las Huertas or the Calle del Arenal, which was later pedestrianized, you can perceive how the venture is transforming unsteady areas into in vogue ones. By introducing presents on keep autos off walkways, making the roads more secure after dull, and renovating old structures, Madrid is striving to make itself increasingly decent.

Simply strolling these vehicle free lanes is by all accounts the manner in which the Madrileños spend their nights. Anybody is allowed to be part of the paseo. Well known courses are along Calle de las Huertas and between Puerta del Sol, the fundamental square, and Court Santa Clause Ana. Indeed, even past 12 PM on a sweltering summer night, whole families with little children are walking, licking frozen yogurt, welcoming their neighbors, and getting a charge out of little brews and tapas in a progression of bars. A most loved neighborhood bite is sautéed pig's ears, and a few bars work in simply that.

Spain boasts of notoriety for celebrating late, holding off on closure until workplaces open toward the beginning of the day. In case you're observing people promptly toward the beginning of the day, it's in reality difficult to tell who is completing their duties and who is simply beginning it. Regardless of whether you're not a hard-core partier after 12 PM, try to stay with the cheerful masses, thriving in the relaxed air.

One explanation individuals remain out late, particularly during the summer, is to get away from the warmth of the day. I frequently contemplate the climate and traffic have nothing else of more noteworthy enthusiasm on their psyches. Be that as it may, here, in the elevated and over-warmed inside of Spain, even individuals with bounty to say talk regarding the climate nowadays. The last summer I spent here, I found myself surveying eateries by the nature of their cooling. I saw poor local people, displaced people from the warmth, lying like reptiles in the shade.

At the point when it's sizzling, Madrileños head to Retiro Park to take an obscure rest in a 300-section of land green-and-windy getaway. It's where you will be able to hopscotch via a mosaic of darlings, families, master seat sitters, skateboarders, and pets strolling their lords.

When the private space of eminence, this glorious park has been a most loved of Madrid's everyday citizens since Ruler Charles III chose to impart it to his subjects in the late eighteenth century. In its middle is a major lake (El Estanque), where you can lease a paddle boat. At early afternoon on Saturday and Sunday, the territory around the lake turns into a road jubilee, with performers, puppeteers, and bunches of neighborhood shading.

Another green desert garden is the Imperial Professional flowerbed (Genuine Jardín Botánico). At this place, you can enjoy a rich and fragrant reprieve in an etched setting, meandering among trees from around the globe. It's in reality in excess of a recreation center — it's a historical center of plants.

For extraordinary perspectives and an antiquated sanctuary, head to the Parque de la Montaña. In 1968, the Egyptian government was appreciative for Spain's assistance in protecting landmarks compromised by transcending the Aswan Dam, so it gave its Sanctuary de Debod to Madrid. Therefore, Madrid is the main spot I can consider in Europe where you can really meander through a flawless unique Egyptian sanctuary — complete with fine cut reliefs from 200 BC. It's in a sentimental park that local people love for its critical displays — particularly at nightfall.

All through Europe, enthusiastic governments are recharging green space and transforming some time ago vehicle clogged badlands into open spaces. To encounter the present Madrid, remove time from the inbuilt sceneries and relish the outside of this bearable city.

Stuffed on the main tram with most people moving towards to the famous Square de Toros, been thinking about how I would respond to watching another session of bullfight. I had not been to one out of 5 years. Finally, everybody heaped out as the elevator siphoned us up straightforwardly to the approaching exterior of the town's field — the greatest in Spain.

It was all crackerjacks and peanuts. The tickets were $8 in light of the fact that the three matadors were simply beginners. Everyone would battle 2 bulls, coming to a total of 6 battles... 2 hours of middle-age man versus mammoth franticness. The male before me in the line of the ticket arranged forcefully for a decent seat. I basically stated, "Uno, por support," and wound up sitting appropriate alongside him.

This late spring, with the sultriest behavior, battles were beginning at nine o'clock. Also, the situation is very dependable. At nine o'clock, more than 450 kilos kilos of furious confused bull surged to the field. Elderly people men took their seat mindfully, as the young ladies vacillated their fans as though excited by the dancing men. Numerous ladies think about bullfighting hot, and welcome running bullfighters, truly dressed to murder in the customary tight jeans. It appeared like anything but difficult to point out who was neighborhood and those who weren't. Visitors pointlessly released camera flashes. And with every murder, neighborhood male croaked "Olé" as the Spanish ladies opted to wave their white handkerchiefs in the air.

The typical bullfight in Spain comprises of 6 bulls, with every custom killing keeps going for twenty minutes. At that point other bull frolics onto the field. You are not liable to watch more blood spillage. In the course of the most recent two hundred years of bullfighting, just a bunch of bullfighters have died. On the off chance that a bull kills a warrior, the following bullfighter arrives to execute the bull. Generally, the mother of the bull is also slaughtered, because the shrewd characteristics are accepted to have originated from her.

With this most recent courtesy call, the executing appeared more disgraceful and coldblooded than any time in recent memory, and the group of spectators, however for the most part Spanish, appeared to incorporate more vacationers than any time in recent memory. After 2 bulls, I decided to leave, feeling somewhat weak as I went past the attendants at the entryway. All of us are travelers. At the tram stage, I remained beside a Midwest family — mother holding little girl's hand as the father held the child's hand. My question was, "Two bulls enough?" The guardians gestured. The child summarized it like this - "That was dreadful."

That was terrible. Not to recognize the significance of the fight is to review an admired piece of Spanish culture. Be that as it may, it additionally makes a display out of the merciless murdering of a creature. Should travelers blacklist bullfights? I don't have a clue. Obviously, notwithstanding going to a bullfight is disputable among basic entitlements fans. I have generally been undecided concerning the scene, feeling that as a movement author, I have to give an account of what exists, as opposed to pass judgment on it and bolster a blacklist. At the point the occasion is maintained by the vacationers, I will rethink my announcing.

Portugal came up with its customized form of the fight. The greatest distinction is the thing that I consider as the Retribution of Toro: The bullfighter is injured alongside the fighting bull.

In the Portuguese tourada's Act 1, the horseman professionally executes a total of 4 beribboned points in the back of the bull, as they attempt to evade the cowhide-cushioned horns. In the second Act, a brightly clad 8-man suicide squad gets into the ring and assembles each record confronting the bull. The pioneer insults the bull as it shouts "touro!" and slaps his knees— at that point prepares himself for a crash that can be heard as far as possible up in the modest seats. He then clings to the head of the bull, and his pals heap on, attempting to fight with the bull to a halt. At long last, one person holds tight to o touro's tail and "water-skis" behind him. (In Act III, the ambulância shows up.)

Dissimilar to the Spanish corrida de toros, the bull isn't slaughtered before the group at the tourada of Portuguese... however it is murdered later. Spanish fans demand that the battles in Portugal are very cruel, because they tend to embarrass the bull, as opposed to battle him as a kindred warrior.

Bullfights in Spain are hung on a number of Sundays nights. Genuine battles with grown-up bullfighters happen from April to the month of October, each year. These are very costly and frequently sold out ahead of time. The battles in summer are regularly novillada, and have expensive tickets, more youthful fighting bulls, and young learners carrying out the executing. No awful seats; and you will get a seat at the shade through paying out for more. The activity regularly deliberately happens in the shade to compensate the expensive holders of the ticket.

It is possible to find a portion of Spanish bullfight "culture" without really heading off to the occasion. Bars all through

Spain are occupied on the bullfight evenings with the activity blasting on the television, and the local group accumulated. In any case, they have an interesting vibe whenever.

My preferred bull bar is spot on Madrid's Court Civic chairman. Its inside is a sanctuary to event, decorated with violent stylistic layout. The amazing activity is caught in a grisly photographic corridor of acclaim covering the divider. For some individuals, a snappy sangria or lager in a resort such as this is all that could possibly be needed awful for their Spanish excursion.

Salamanca's Court City hall leader, Spain's most excellent square, appears to praise life. Walking around the square with Carlos, my guide, we passed a youngster strolling alone who all of a sudden burst into melody. I asked Carlos for what valid reason and he stated, "Doesn't it happen where you live?"

Northwest of Madrid (three hours via train), Salamanca is young and untouristy, showing its relentless landmarks, groups of shelters, and glorious square with calm pride.

Carlos and I took a seat at a table with a prime perspective on the square and every one of its kin activity. Carlos requested us a straightforward however rich dinner: a plate of restored ham, patatas bravas (pieces of potatoes with tomato sauce) and glasses of strong neighborhood red wine. At the point when the ham showed up, he recounted his grandpa daintily cutting a jamón, bolstered in a jamonero (ham holder) during Christmas, painting an occasion picture that helped me to remember my father cutting the turkey at Thanksgiving.

Our view was loaded up with individuals. Court City hall leader has for some time been Salamanca's people group lounge room. The most significant spot around the local area, it is by all accounts constantly facilitating some sort of gathering. Spaniards love their paseo (evening walk) — it resembles multi-generational "cruising" without autos. While the old-clocks meddled and "tsk-tsked" at the wanton youngsters, those youthful singles were out to see and be seen. Carlos clarified that generally, the square is a major review field where the men course one way and the ladies circle the other so everybody gets an opportunity to look at everybody. Being a tease seethes as the young men are on a journey for the ideal queso (cheddar), which means an adorable dish. Maybe the best time of for people-viewing is Sunday after Mass, when the grandmas assemble here in their Sunday best.

The Square Civic chairman is only the beginning stage for a Salamanca visit. Salamanca's college, the most seasoned in Spain (from around 1218), was one of Europe's driving focuses of learning for a long time. Columbus came here for movement tips. Today numerous Americans make the most of its incredible summer program. The old auditoriums around the focal house, where huge numbers of Spain's Brilliant Age legends contemplated, are available to the general population. A portion of the rooms are as yet utilized by the college for esteemed scholastic functions. The passageway entrance of the college is an incredible case of Spain's Plateresque style (Spain's variant of Ostentatious Gothic) — the style named for stone work so mind boggling it would appear that silverwork.

In the college's Corridor of Conflict Luis de León, the tables and seats are made of tight wooden pillars, trimmed somewhere near a very long time of studious doodling. The teacher used to talk from the congregation undermining catedra (platform). It was here that freethinking Quarrel Luis de León enraged Probe powers by getting the sacred writings to the individuals their very own language. In the wake of being imprisoned and tormented for a long time, he came back to his place and began his first post-detainment address with, "As we were saying..."

Close to the college stands the Congregation of San Esteban, committed to St. Stephen (Esteban) the saint. The congregation contains great orders, a pantheon of tombs, and an exhibition hall with represented sixteenth century ensemble books. However, everything is overpowered by the congregation's Churriguera altarpiece, a typical case of the style named after the craftsman. Unobtrusively contemplate the gold-plated curds as visitors shake their heads and state "to an extreme" in their primary language.

Salamanca's numerous understudies help hold costs down. The youngsters assemble under the stars until late in the night, reciting and cheering, talking and singing. Throughout the hundreds of years, the college's more unfortunate understudies earned cash to finance their training by singing in Salamanca's roads: a custom called "fish music." The name fish, which has nothing to do with fish, alludes to a drifter understudy lifestyle and later was applied to the music these understudies sing. This fifteenth to eighteenth century custom endures today as gatherings of understudies, wearing the conventional dark capes and stockings, sing and play mandolins and guitars, serenading the general population in the bars close by the Court City hall leader. While they make their genuine cash performing for weddings on ends of the week, you're probably going to see them out singing for tips on summer week evenings.

For a fun feast, do the tapa tango. Salamanca bars offer an incredible determination of tapas, including a delectable assortment of treats — fish, plates of mixed greens, meat-filled cakes, rotisserie treats, unendingly. Wash down your tapa with frosted gazpacho (zesty tomato soup), a cool treat on a hot day.

Try not to miss the charms of the bright sandstone city of Salamanca — with Spain's most stupendous court, its most established college, and an interesting history all swaddled in a reasonable and carefree school town vibe.

Acknowledgements

Thank you for making it through to the end of *Spain travel guide: an unusual and evocative journey across Spain*, let's hope it was informative and able to provide you with all of the tools you need to achieve your goals in Spain whatever they may be.

The next step is to go there in person!

Bonus chapter:

Essential tips for first-time visitors to the Canary Islands

By Andres Arias

What is the best about Canary Islands?

The Canary Islands are differed to such an extent that selecting them one of the best is an outlandish task. The beneficial thing about this is regardless of what your travel style is, there'll be an island that suits your requirements.

Are you searching for a great deal of nature to ogle at? A spot to pull up and unwind on the seashore? Some place to get dynamic? We have you secured with our manual for the best Canary Islands for you.

For a smidgen of everything: Tenerife

There is the reason manufactured hotels, for example, Playa de las Americas and Costa Adeje, at that point there's the remainder of island; a lot greater part, where most Canarias have lived for five centuries.

What Tenerife offers is a decent variety. It's enormous enough to be home to cosmopolitan urban areas with memorable focuses, clamoring towns, little towns, provincial farmlands and colossal breadths of National Park where you can stroll around.

It additionally flaunts the most elevated mountain in Spain, the transcending Mount Teide, whose sheer mass gives an astounding prologue to guests landing via air. Also, obviously, practically everywhere throughout the island, some mind-blowing seashores for all preferences. Like Gran Canaria, Tenerife, the biggest island of the Canaries, brags an enormous assortment mountain, backwoods, and seashore scenes with an ever-warm atmosphere.

Most remarkably, it contains the lofty Mount Teide, a monstrous well of lava which, at 3,718 meters, is the most elevated top in the entirety of Spain and the third biggest fountain of liquid magma on the planet. . There are various climbing trails that grandstand a perspective on an extraterrestrial scene. The biggest of the Canaries is likewise the most well-known with voyagers.

The most astounding thing about the seashores in Tenerife are the stretches of thick, black sand found on a few, for instance on Playa de El Puertito and Playa del Roque on the eastern coast. In the city of Santa Cruz de Tenerife, two seashores merit visiting: Las Teresitas, a fake seashore with 1,500 meters of sand taken from the Sahara Desert, and Las Gaviotas, a momentous bare seashore with dark sand. For exceptional waves and significantly more chances to get out bare, look at the delightful, difficult to-get to seashores of Playa de los Patos and Playa de Bollullo.

Arriving: Tenerife has two air terminals, Los Rodeos air terminal in the north and the Reina Sofia air terminal in the south. Most universal flights get through the Reina Sofia air terminal, while between island flights land at Los Rodeos. Ships land at the city of Santa Cruz from Gran Canaria, La Palma, and Fuerteventura.

For wind-sport lovers and seashore bums: Fuerteventura

The second biggest of the Canary Islands lies not exactly a hundred kilometers from the African coast and it is one of the least created. Fuerteventura is a dry desert-like departure whose east coast is the primary fascination, where the moving sands of Corralejo and Jandia blown in on the Saharan breeze.

Fuerteventura is the seashore heaven of the islands, with the Corralejo hills more like a smaller than usual Sahara than a seashore. Fuerteventura's retreats can be fairly ailing in enchant, the magnificence gave by brilliant sands and turquoise oceans.

Corralejo, in the north, is the stand apart hotel and a major supporter of making Fuerteventura a standout amongst other Canary Islands. Here British families blend – in a resort that is likewise a genuine Spanish town – with local people, surfers and windsurfers from everywhere throughout the world.

There are little tapas bars, extravagant cafés and appropriate seashores directly nearby. Jandia, in the south, is progressively prevalent with German guests. The principle resort Morro Jable is home to an epic 4km seashore yet know there are extends where garments are undoubtedly discretionary. Somewhere else on Fuerteventura you'll discover volcanoes to climb, minimal whitewashed inland towns and the delectable Majorero cheddar, best delighted in barbecued with a little palm nectar.

The most established of the Canaries, this island is known for its kilometers-long seashores of white sand and shallow, clear water, ideal for water-skiing, windsurfing, angling, or cruising. It has the longest coastline of each of the seven islands, spreading over 340 kilometers, and is effectively available by a 40-minute ship from Lanzarote.

Arriving: Flights come into Fuerteventura Airport, 5 km outside of Puerto del Rosario, from different islands and from most significant European urban communities. Ships land at Corralejo from Lanzarote, Tenerife, and Gran Canaria.

For a spread of landscapes: Gran Canaria

Gran Canaria experiences a similar picture as Tenerife regularly expelled as meager in excess of a mass the travel industry goal. In actuality, it's actually the equivalent, with the most fascinating parts to be found outside of the retreats. Amusingly, the two islands are very comparable in character in spite of the savage contention between them.

The individuals who like Tenerife should, in principle, similar to Gran Canaria in spite of the fact that there are contrasts. Gran Canaria has better seashores, Las Palmas conceals Santa Cruz with regards to appealing verifiable quarters, an awesome city sea shore in Las Canteras and a flourishing unrecorded music scene.

Inland towns on Gran Canaria are simpler on the eye than those on Tenerife and the view is increasingly epic, nearly Arizona-like in parts. The islanders guarantee the best perspectives on Tenerife's super fountain of liquid magma, regardless of whether they don't have Mount Teide with its entrancing volcanic eruption.

The "Landmass in Miniature" traveler office appellation for this conveniently round island is, for once, no exaggeration; Gran Canaria offers more picturesque decent variety than any of different islands, popping it high on the rundown of the best Canary Islands.

There are the epic sands of Maspalomas in the south, the subtropical woods of the inside, tough mountains and, in Las Palmas, the most overwhelming of the island capitals with its humming nightlife and sandy seashores. Gran Canaria is a major climbing goal, as well, with a system of well-stamped trails and a mobile celebration.

The island likewise delivers better than average wine and the brilliant Tropical ale – immaculate to end a long climb. The most youthful of the seven primary islands, beautiful Lanzarote is likewise the most stylishly satisfying – to a great extent on account of one man.

Lanzarote-conceived, he went through a large portion of his time on earth on the island and made an inheritance that guests can get familiar with at his old studio home, which presently houses the César Manrique Foundation.

Volcanic movement has additionally prompted an interesting viticulture that sees scrumptious Malaysia developed in the island's volcanic holes. You can visit the bunch of well-kept wineries to get limited jugs or appreciate them in the rich spread of eateries that have made the island prominent with foodies.

Somewhere else you'll locate a supernatural volcanic getaway in Timanfaya National Park, while the island of La Graciosa is a laidback street free hideaway. Lanzarote's most appealing retreat is family benevolent Playa Blanca in the south, with the fundamental fascination the well-known white sand seashores that give it its name.

The most unprecedented sights on this island are its precarious gorges of stone shake, which dive from just about 2,000 meters high to meet the coastline. From pretty much anyplace you can value the sheer power of nature that Gran Canaria brings to the table.

You can investigate an assortment of vegetation in regions like Tejeda, with its rich green valleys of almond trees, and Mogan, a valley where tropical natural products are developed. There are additionally many angling towns worth visiting for their precipitous ocean perspectives and community engage, for example, Agaete and Arinaga. In the antiquated city of Arucas, gigantic banana estates, rough bays, and volcanic territories structure neighboring scenes.

Remember about the unending white sand seashores and turquoise waters, which can be delighted in Maspalomas, situated alongside a territory of sand rises, and furthermore in Playa del Inglés, the two of which make up the more prominent zones for sea shore going. For calmer sea shores and pretty bays, attempt La Costa de Bañaderos or Playa de las Nieves, the two of which offer unfathomable mountain sees.

Arriving: Flights roll in from most significant European urban communities and from different islands to Gran Canaria Airport, 16 km south of the city of Las Palmas. Ships to the city of Las Palmas are accessible from Lanzarote, Tenerife, La Palma, and Fuerteventura.

For stunning landscape: La Palma

Known as La Isla Bonita, La Palma is, as the name proposes, perhaps the prettiest of the Canary Islands. It has history, Santa Cruz de la Palma was a shipbuilding port in the days when explorers crossed the sea to the New World and privateers wandered these parts. Furthermore, it has excellent landscape you won't discover on other Canary Islands .

It is no big surprise that the most northwesterly of the isles is known as the "Lovely Island". The whole island has been proclaimed an UNESCO biosphere hold for its swathe of surprising landscape: a few sections are significantly volcanic and others rich rainforest – and if that is not an explanation La Palma is a standout amongst other Canary Islands to visit, we don't have the foggiest idea what is. The grand feature is the Caldera de Taburiente National Park where the best perspectives on the archipelago can be seen from Roque de los Muchachos at 2396m.

You can drive more than halfway up and afterward meander around this volcanic hill by walking. The capital, Santa Cruz de la Palma, is an alluring notable jolt gap on the sea that is definitely justified even despite a day or two of investigation.

Arriving: Direct flights to La Palma air terminal in the city of Santa Cruz de La Palma are accessible from terrain Spain, different islands, and a few urban communities in northern

Europe. Ships land in Santa Cruz de La Palma from Tenerife and Gran Canaria

For an all-out break: El Hierro

The most enchanted and puzzling island of all, El Hierro was at one time the island at the edge of the world. There is as yet a specific riddle noticeable all around; it's simply not exactly like different islands.

There is a fantastical Sabine backwoods, an unusual minimal old settlement dissimilar to any somewhere else on the Canaries, goliath reptiles and an inn that was at one time the littlest on Earth.

The jumping should be the best of the considerable number of islands though the slopes, with their groups of wooly sheep and dry-stone dividers, can now and then feel more Yorkshire than an island near Africa. An absence of air traffic and a three-hour ship ride keeps guest numbers low, making El Hierro at the edge of the Canary Islands world genuinely meriting the term 'pristine'.

A level and rugged territory make up the focal piece of the island, where ascends as the most noteworthy pinnacle. From here, you can respect the perspectives on the bay, woodlands, volcanic cavities, and of the whole island.

The coast likewise offers an entrancing and new sight with its precipices sticking away from under the water, as though they were little bluff islands. El Golfo is the place the biggest measure of precipices can be found alongside the absolute most elevated perspectives of the region.

Arriving: Flights come into the little air terminal at Valverde from Tenerife and Gran Canaria , no universal flights. Ships land at La Estaca harbor from Tenerife.

Made in United States
North Haven, CT
09 December 2021